STAYING BOTHERED

Find Your Passion, Commit to Action, Change the World

Jamie C. Amelio
with Adam Snyder

HybridGlobal
PUBLISHING

Published by
Hybrid Global Publishing
301 E 57th Street, 4th fl
New York, NY 10022

Manufactured in the United States of America, or in the United Kingdom when distributed elsewhere.

Amelio, Jamie C.
   Staying Bothered: Find Your Passion, Commit to Action,
   Change the World
   LCCN: 2019940071
   ISBN: 978-1-948181-59-4 (hardcover)
         978-1-948181-64-8 (softcover)
         978-1-948181-60-0 (e-book)

Cover design by: Joe Potter
Interior design: Claudia Volkman

ACKNOWLEDGMENTS

Because of the support I have been given, through days of pain, betrayal, hope, and humor, I believe I am the luckiest lady alive, with the best job on the planet.

My deepest thanks to each of the thousands of volunteers who have given their heart and soul to Caring for Cambodia.

To my family, and that includes friends who are really family, I am so grateful. Writing a book is hard. Having people you trust with your life is a gift. Adam and Pat Snyder have been exactly that.

To my children. They are the inspiration that pushes me every day to Stay Bothered. May you never give up, and follow your dreams even when the clouds roll in and the sun is far off.

And of course to Bill, my husband, my rock. Thank you for supporting me every day with my projects and commitments that keep me bothered, and for loving and understanding me.

TABLE OF CONTENTS

TO THE READER

—⚬⚬⚬—

I've been bothered most of my life. I don't mean bothered about everyday annoyances, like getting cut off in traffic, washing your new white shirt with your equally new blue jeans, getting the wrong order at Starbucks, or having your teenage daughter leave a half-eaten slice of pizza on her nightstand for two weeks—*again*. I'm talking about Big Things—the fact that science has yet to find a cure for cancer, or that 1,600 children die each day from diseases directly linked to unsafe drinking water.

I've long believed that being bothered is a good thing—as long as you're able to identify what bothers you, do something about it, and *stay bothered*. Success comes to those who try. And try. And keep trying.

These ideas were driven home to me sixteen years ago when my family and I were living in Singapore and I visited Cambodia for the first time. I saw children who had to pay to go to school but couldn't afford it because their parents made less money in a day than Americans pay for a cup of coffee. Many of those who did attend school often arrived hungry. We changed this paradigm for thousands of Cambodian children. With the help of an equal number of volunteers from all over the world, Caring for Cambodia (CFC) today feeds and educates 6,700 students each year, from preschool to high school, in twenty-one new buildings. We were able to do it because collectively we found what bothered us, did something about it, and stayed bothered.

I described the genesis and growth of CFC in *Graced with Orange: How Caring for Cambodia Changed Lives, Including My Own*, published in 2012. What began as a promise to a little girl to visit her school grew into a larger promise to provide a world-class education to the children of Siem Reap. Our model schools and our teacher training program have revolutionized an entire country's education system.

This book, *Staying Bothered: Find Your Passion, Commit to Action, Change the World,* is written with the goal of sharing what I've learned about **finding a personal cause and sticking to it. It is a personal memoir, but I hope it's also a call to action.** Based on the growing population of our website, stayingbothered.com, I believe it can become a movement.

Discovering what really bothers you is a magical experience, but *staying bothered* leads to growth and change—for you and the rest of the world. **Being bothered is easy; staying bothered is hard but life-changing.** I'm not suggesting that you wallow in negativity by focusing exclusively on the atrocities that occur all over the world every day. You have a life. But I *am* hoping you can make the difficult choice to pay attention to your bothers, particularly those staring you in the face.

A bother is always personal; that's why you feel it so strongly. When it hits close to home, its passion is intensified. That's what happened to me when my sixteen-year-old needed help overcoming depression and anxiety. Just like that, teen mental health became my new bother. I'll talk about this in the final chapter.

All of us face personal and professional challenges. The common thread is how we use perseverance, mixed with gratitude and a dash of serendipity, to improve our lives and the lives of those around us. By staying bothered, we can learn a lot about ourselves and our place in the universe.

This book is about finding what bothers you the most, facing it head-on, and being reinvigorated rather than dismayed by the challenges and obstacles that inevitably occur—not *if* they come your way, but *when.* In those moments, let go of the failure. Your job during the tough times is to **find something, anything, that is good.** Build on that; focus on it every day. Find something in your life you can own: a feeling, a workout, a certain path. **Take it and own it, because you control it.**

PROLOGUE

AN ACCIDENT
(OR WAS IT A BLESSING?)

For thirty-seven years, I innocently referred to it as the "accident."

One late afternoon in August 1981, I was driving too fast on FM Road 1518, a bucolic two-lane road in my hometown of Schertz, Texas, twenty-two miles northeast of San Antonio. I was behind the wheel of the 1979 Plymouth Road Runner my dad had bought me a few months earlier. For a sixteen-year-old, the car was nearly perfect—light blue and full of muscle and power—until I drove it, head-on, into one of the many sprawling oak trees that lined the road. Inside the car, the collision sounded like a clap of thunder. My body slammed against the steering wheel, the impact crushing my ribs and piercing my liver and spleen.

I should have died that day. I managed to open the door and crawl to the edge of the road, where a man found me and called an ambulance. I was in surgery for six hours. I can clearly recall the overhead lights in the operating room, the sound of my parents crying, and the dozens of staples the doctors used to hold my body together.

I've always called it the "accident," but that word fails to capture the impact it had on my life. When you look up antonyms for *accident* in a thesaurus, one of the first words you come across is *blessing*. That seems more appropriate. I was granted a second chance, and I intended to make the most of it.

Thirty-eight years later I would be given the same sort of wake-up call. The evening of February 22, 2015, started out like most Sunday nights at the Amelio house. Our fourteen-year-old son, Bronson, and his ten-year-old sister, Avery, were working on their homework—or at least they were supposed to be. Jes, my eldest son Austin's girlfriend, was in the family room watching television. Their one-year-old son Lev was already asleep for the night. The rest of us were rushing to finish whatever personal tasks we needed to do before *The Walking Dead* began. Austin had joined the cast that season, and although he wasn't going to appear on that night's episode, we had become huge fans.

As I had been doing for months, I gave myself an injection of the antiaging hormone, HGH, that my doctor had prescribed. For the past three years I'd been giving Avery two allergy shots every other day, so any misgivings I might have had about needles, I'd lost long before. Thankfully, as it turned out, Avery had become equally comfortable. "It's okay, Mom," she often told me. "I'm not squeamish."

I had no fears about the medication I was taking, or my health. I was forty-nine years old, worked out regularly, took daily vitamins, and was careful about what I ate. But minutes after taking the medication, I could tell something wasn't right. My lips started to tingle, as if a thousand acupuncture needles had been inserted into them. I began to lose feeling in my hands. I tried to reach for the Benadryl we kept in the kitchen cabinet. As I did, everything slowed down.

I stumbled into the family room, where Jes was watching television. I believe I said that something was wrong with me, but maybe I was only thinking it. My chest was getting tighter and tighter. I couldn't breathe. I needed to lie down. Everything was starting to fade. My husband, Bill, walked in and immediately noticed I wasn't looking so good. I would have fallen to the floor if he hadn't grabbed me and helped me to lie down. I could hear people talking, but I couldn't understand what they were saying. I wanted to tell Bill what was wrong, but I couldn't get the words out. Even if I could have, I don't know what I would have said. Bill said it for me: "This is serious. I'm calling 911."

I tried to concentrate on my body. The tingling sensation was now in my legs and spreading upward. Soon it became harder to breathe. My chest felt like it was frozen. I couldn't get air in or out. My body was telling me I could stop breathing, that I could relax and let go. With my mind's eye, I could see something colorful and calm, beyond the here and now. It was beautiful. For a moment, I thought about giving up, but that seemed ridiculous.

Jes was really upset and Avery was shouting. Bill's body language suggested he must be shouting too. He told Avery to get the EpiPen. She was the only one who knew how to use it and exactly where we kept it: up high in a cabinet where Lev couldn't reach. On the phone, Bill confirmed with the emergency personnel that he should administer the EpiPen.

Avery knew just what to do. For years, Bill and I had been drilling into her the idea that in case of an emergency, an EpiPen could save her life. We had rehearsed how to use it many times, both at the doctor's office and at home. The practice pen even produced a small prick in the skin, just like a real needle.

I imagined I was mind melding with my beautiful youngest child, but in reality, Avery acted alone. She grabbed the EpiPen, reached back with her right arm, and—*wham!*— jammed it into my thigh.

Almost immediately I'm feeling a warm sensation move down my leg and simultaneously inside my head. Avery has saved my life! Or has she? I still can't breathe. The strangest thoughts envelop me. I am hovering in the air. I look down on a room of strangers. Firemen and paramedics scurry in and out. There is ordered confusion, which ends with me being transported in an EMS ambulance. Inside the vehicle Bill watches me go from bad to worse. A man in a blue uniform says my pulse is very slow. Someone says I should rest. But I don't need rest; I need strength. So I pray.

Praying comes easily because I do it regularly, in church and on my own. I prayed for Austin when he was in recovery; for our son Riley when he had knee surgery; for our son Bronson, when he had surgery to fix his jaw; for Avery when she almost drowned in the lake by our house; for

Cherry and Rathana, the two Cambodian girls we helped raise when they came to America knowing very little English; and for Bill whenever he boarded a plane or helicopter.

I pray, but I don't ask to be saved. Instead, it is, "God, if you want me, I'll go." Strange how this is so clear to me and not at all frightening. Like a strobe light, these words flash in my head more times than I can count: "God, if you want me, I'll go."

By the time we got to the hospital, my body had been returned to me. This wasn't the end after all. I had more to do, a life to live, kids to help. So many kids.

Since that day, I've read a lot about near-death, out-of-body experiences, and I've watched plenty of films on the subject. I'm a sucker for movies like *Heaven Is for Real* and *Hereafter*. The experiences described are remarkably similar, involving the sensation of floating outside your body and witnessing it from a perspective removed from yourself. But these stories always featured someone else. Now it had happened to me.

The world looks different afterwards. I observed firsthand life's fragility and my own mortality. In that moment, I thought I was dying. I was *certain* I was dying. Like the details of a dream that can't be resurrected, much of what occurred during those twenty minutes remains out of reach. Still, I was left with something real. In the days and months that followed, I hardly talked about the experience. Even after Bill researched what must have happened—an allergic reaction to the HGH—I didn't want to discuss it. Yet I still think about the incident often. It was a reminder that the philosophy I had adopted more than a decade before—staying bothered—was one worth fighting for. It was a wake-up call. Almost dying made me fiercer. I learned that I have more than enough energy to take on the issues that bother me the most. Now, if I have something to say, I say it! If I have something to do, I do it! And if I have wisdom to share, I share it! That's what inspired me to write this book.

ONE

——◦/◦/◦——

FIND YOUR BOTHER

I discovered my bother, the issue that would become my life's mission, in January 2003, soon after Bill became the president of Dell's Asia-Pacific region. We were living in Singapore when I visited Cambodia for the first time with my best friend, Virginia, and her daughter, Amanda. In Siem Reap, a city of approximately a quarter of a million people in northwestern Cambodia, we visited the magnificent temples of Angkor Wat, the centerpiece of the Khmer kingdom from the ninth to the fifteenth centuries. As we were watching a group of monks in bright orange robes walk across the temple grounds, a little girl tugged on my sleeve and asked me in perfect English for a dollar.

"What's your name?" I asked, "and how will you use the dollar?"

"My name is Srelin, and I need the dollar so I can go to school."

The cynic in me thought, *What a clever way to fleece tourists*, but I agreed to give her the dollar—as long as she showed me her school. That was the beginning of a forty-eight-hour period that would change the course of my life. It was also the first of what we began calling "orange moments," those moments when individuals "get" what CFC is trying to do in Cambodia. I have repeatedly witnessed peoples' inner light turn a brilliant orange when they walk into one of our classrooms, hold the hand of a young Cambodian student, or congratulate an older student on his or her success. This was *my* turn, the first of many.

That afternoon we visited Srelin's school in Kravaan. More than seventy-five children of all ages were crammed into a small, poorly lit classroom with a dirt floor. As many as four or five were forced to sit at the same narrow desk. Some students were sharing a small chair. Their only school supplies were pencils, many of which were broken into small pieces so everyone could have one. When we entered the classroom, the children stared in wonder at the three American women, all of us patiently waiting for a teacher who would never arrive.

Children at Kravaan School

What I saw bothered me. It also occurred to me that it wouldn't take all that much to make a genuine difference in Cambodia, a country still recovering from the genocide the Khmer Rouge carried out between 1975 and 1979. During these terrible years, in the name of creating an agrarian utopia, the Khmer Rouge killed an estimated two million Cambodians, a quarter of the population, in a wave of murder, torture, and starvation aimed particularly at the educated and intellectual elite. If you wore glasses, you were in danger.

In 2003 I had scant knowledge of any of this. What I did see, however, left a powerful impression on me. I could have returned to my busy life in Singapore and forgotten what I had witnessed. I could have focused all my attention on being a good wife and mother. That's enough, right? But I was too bothered to do that, a feeling that has never left me.

Before leaving Kravaan, I learned that many students did have to pay their teachers. I told our guide I wanted to pay for Srelin and a few other children to attend school for the remainder of the year. It wasn't much, but it was a start. That's how Caring for Cambodia was born— not from a desire to micromanage the lives of others or a need to make my already busy days more hectic, but from a sense that something was wrong and I could help provide a solution. Its origins can be traced to my feelings about the perils Srelin and all the other children like her in Cambodia faced when it came to getting an education. The situation bothered me, and that bother motivated me to do something. Once I had made that commitment, there was only one other question to answer: would I *stay* bothered?

Caring for Cambodia

The story of how in just sixteen years Caring for Cambodia became so established and influential in Cambodia is more complicated than how we got started. How did we go from operating out of a ramshackle, one-room schoolhouse to having forty-two new buildings at twenty-one schools, 280 newly trained teachers, and feeding two meals per day to 6,700 students? What did we do to prompt the Cambodian Ministry of Education to endorse CFC's brand of teaching as a model to be emulated by the rest of the country?

My best explanation is that I wasn't the only who got bothered and stayed that way. The biggest factor in our early success was the creation of a sustainable volunteer organization in Singapore. We were able to get people there excited about helping children in a developing country just two hours by air but, in nearly every other regard, light years away. Every month someone would offer to host a fundraiser or volunteer to lick stamps and fill backpacks. As soon as we lost one volunteer, another would arrive to fill the empty position.

Aranh campus before and after MAD trip

Our volunteers come from all walks of life. They cover the political spectrum, from the most conservative to the most liberal. We've had grandparents volunteer, as well as small children, heirs to small fortunes, and people living paycheck to paycheck. The one trait they all have in common is that they were not only bothered when they first heard about the education system in Cambodia, but they stayed bothered. Even after returning to their everyday lives, they didn't let the feeling fade.

It seemed like five minutes after my return to Singapore from that first trip to Cambodia, my house was crowded with volunteers filling backpacks with donated notebooks, pencils, toothbrushes, soap, and school uniforms. Two weeks later I made my second trip to Siem Reap with a few friends, and we distributed the backpacks to every student at Srelin's school. Soon we were organizing Make a Difference (MAD) trips, which now bring more than seven hundred volunteers from all over the world to Cambodia each year to build playgrounds, homes, even entire schools. We've torn down dilapidated buildings and built new ones in their place. We've painted, and painted, and painted some more, creating vibrant, lively classrooms and libraries. During our first year we put special emphasis on making our schools places where learning is fun and exciting. Soon the children's colorful artwork began to cover the walls, supplemented by playful presentations of numbers and letters imported from Singapore.

The first school we built from the ground up was in Spien Chrieve, one of the poorest villages in the area despite being just 20 kilometers south of the country's top tourist attraction, the temples of Angkor Wat. In 2003 the school was a rundown, one-room structure with dirt for a floor. Now it is a sprawling campus with a new cafeteria, library, teacher training center, and twelve child-friendly classrooms where trained teachers are actively engaged and supported. The new buildings we erected succeeded in making the teachers and students feel completely different about their schools. Classrooms where students once had to duck under a table when it rained were replaced by modern learning centers.

Original Spien Chrieve School, before CFC and little girl hiding under a desk

The momentum was self-generating. Before I had a chance to blink, we were a registered nongovernmental organization (NGO). We were not only building schools, but also training teachers and feeding and educating students in a manner not typically seen in Cambodia. Starting CFC opened my eyes to just how generous people can be. When people weren't giving us their time, they were donating money.

I think a lot of people stop being bothered as soon as they realize that to create lasting change, they can't do it alone. You might not have the means to start an organization like I did. It takes a tremendous amount of time, energy, and fundraising. But that shouldn't stop you. You can join an organization that already exists or start something small in your own community. The desire to give is universal; it's impossible to stereotype those who do it most often. You can be Christian or atheist, Muslim or Jew. You can have all the money in the world, or very little. The father of one of my good friends gives fifteen dollars to CFC every month. We also have people who have written a check for $100,000. The figures might vary, but the level of generosity is the same. The only common denominator is becoming bothered and staying that way.

You don't need to have a CEO husband or the wherewithal to fly around the world. You can have a tremendous impact on your bother, whatever it may be, no matter who you are or where you live. I did not set out to become a CEO, and I've learned a few things along the way:

- Educate yourself. Once I found my bother, I learned everything I could about Cambodia, about educating children, about running an NGO. Watch TED Talks. Listen to podcasts. Emulate leaders you admire. Take their ideas and use them; there is no need to reinvent the wheel.

- Let go of your failures. Move on and learn.

- Build relationships. You'll never get anywhere alone.

- Stay away from people who belittle your ambitions. Great people make you feel great; then you become great.

- Don't start something if you are unwilling to lead.

- You'll run into people who are mean, impatient, and spiteful. Be kind anyway.

- Learn how to say thank you in a million different ways. And mean it.

- Don't take life too seriously. You cannot change everything. Change *something* and keep on going.

TWO

——⟨⟩——

GO DEEP, NOT WIDE

Once you find your bother, be open to the idea that it need not remain exactly the same over the years. Just as you change and evolve, so will your bother.

But not too much. You will always be you, and pretending you are something else is not going to work. Let me tell you what I mean in very practical terms.

One way we describe our mission at CFC is that we "go deep, not wide." This means focusing our efforts on developing and improving the schools we already have, rather than exhausting our energy looking for new projects that don't reflect our mission. We remain conscious about avoiding "charity drift," the sneaky but almost inevitable desire to steer a nonprofit organization in a new direction. We know we can't adopt every school in Cambodia, just as we can't feed every hungry child. But by making our schools and teachers the best they can possibly be, we can show the rest of the country how education is the most important step on the path that leads out of poverty.

There are more than twelve thousand public schools in Cambodia. We're in charge of twenty-one of them. Our goal was never to take control of the country's entire education system. Rather, it is to use the handful of schools we operate in Siem Reap as an example of what's possible. We train teachers, feed students, and improve infrastructure. We go deep by teaching gender equity, healthy lifestyles, and twenty-first-century skills. We want our standard of education to become the de facto model for preschool to twelfth-grade education across Cambodia, with the ultimate aim of handing over operational responsibilities to individual communities.

One of the best examples of how we go deep is our longstanding effort to improve the health of our students. It's no secret in Cambodia that CFC students are healthier than those who attend government-run schools. It's also no secret why. In addition to providing two nutritious meals a day, we encourage our students to adopt good habits, such as washing their hands before meals and brushing their teeth afterwards. Every new CFC student undergoes vision, hearing, and dental screenings. Their height, weight, and body mass index are recorded and monitored throughout their school careers. When we identify those with vision or hearing problems, the simplest solution—moving them to the front of the classroom—often works best, although we have also fitted hundreds of students with glasses. We refer students in need of more radical intervention to our partner healthcare providers.

CFC vision screenings

At the same time we go deep and not wide, CFC also takes a broad view of our educational responsibilities. We do not see this as a contradiction.

CFC students learning about organic gardening and robotics

Teaching the curriculum with an eye toward the national exam is important, but so are the programs we've pioneered. As we empower teachers through intensive training and mentoring, the goal is to transfer that power to the students. Programs such as career corner, gender equality, information and communications technology, robotics, organic gardening, and carpentry are all aimed at giving students life skills that encourage them to become successful members of their communities.

Girls Matter!

In 2013 we launched our Girls Matter! program. School enrollment for girls in Cambodia plummets between the sixth grade and the start of

Girls Matter! at CFC schools

high school. The reason is straightforward. Staying home to do chores and care for younger siblings benefits their families, while remaining in school hurts them, at least in the short-term. Transportation to and from school, books, uniforms, and sometimes tuition all cost money. According to a recent UNESCO report, almost a quarter of all Cambodian students are forced to give up school and go to work. Most of those students are girls.

Hoping to break the pattern, we are teaching families in Cambodia that a lack of education correlates with ongoing poverty, an absence of self-determination, and a vulnerability to abuse and exploitation. Our counselors work with girls and boys during their secondary school years to help them resolve problems and engage them in conversations about gender issues. By carving out time in the school day and prompting community-wide discussions, we are giving our girls the courage to stay in school, gain the leadership skills necessary to capitalize on their education, and seek the same career opportunities as boys.

The importance of our Girls Matter! program becomes clear when you consider how common it is in Cambodia for sex traffickers to exploit girls and young women. We became fully aware of this problem several years ago when a man showed up at one of our schools with his niece. He told us the girl's parents had died and she was now living with her newly married aunt, whose husband intended to sell her to the highest bidder. The chef at our school in Aranh took her in and welcomed her as part of her family. She is now enjoying her senior year in high school.

Like several of my colleagues, at first I didn't love the name "Girls Matter!" I preferred "Gender Equality." I've changed my mind, though. Girls Matter! clearly states the program's mission and has been effective in our outreach efforts, even drawing the attention of Michelle Obama. While campaigning for gender equality around the world as first lady, in March 2015 she visited our students in Siem Reap, creating quite a buzz throughout all our schools.

Michelle Obama visiting CFC schools

In 2015 our Girls Matter! program was honored by Women for Women Ohio (W4WO) at a new museum on the campus of Kent State University. Ever since May 4, 1970, when members of the Ohio National Guard shot and killed four students protesting the U.S. bombing of Cambodia, Kent State has been indelibly linked to Cambodia. In 2010, inspired by the best-selling book by Nicholas

Kristof and Sheryl WuDunn, *Half the Sky: Turning Oppression into Opportunity for Women Worldwide*, W4WO began to research ways to help women in developing countries. Since then, it has contributed to CFC's Girls Matter! program every year.

In April 2016 I was invited by W4WO to share the dais with Loung Ung, the author of *First They Killed My Father*, which in 2017 Angelina Jolie turned into a feature film. In the book Loung describes her experiences living in Cambodia after the Khmer Rouge assumed power. Her six siblings were sent to labor camps, while she was trained as a child soldier. Loung and I immediately hit it off, at first in no small part because she's a big fan of *The Walking Dead*. We were a good one-two punch. She talked about "what happened then," and I concentrated on "what can happen now."

Teacher Training

Early on, our biggest hurdle as an organization was finding committed, qualified teachers. During the Khmer Rouge years, 75 percent of the country's more than twenty thousand teachers were killed. Fifty of the 725 university instructors survived. No wonder our teachers were inexperienced. They were part of a generation that had seen the Khmer Rouge outlaw public school education. They had grown up in an era in which they more likely had been taught to shoot a gun than to read and write. One of our best teachers, Chan Vandy, learned the Khmer alphabet by using a rock to scrape words in the dirt.

In 2002 most of our teachers had a low opinion of their profession, which was reflected in their performance and in the appearance of their classrooms. As in most government schools, they tended to show up late—if they bothered to come at all. Collectively they had no memory of being valued by the government or by their communities. Their classrooms were overcrowded and ill-equipped. The government rarely paid them on time, which contributed to their demoralization.

During CFC's first year, our Education Committee met twice a week in Singapore, posing questions and brainstorming about the issues we faced. One of our most important early decisions was to give our teachers a stipend so they could count on a steady wage. Another was to give bonuses to the best of them and appoint four Cambodian mentor teachers to supervise them all. We implemented three different pay scales, factoring in the salary teachers received from the government, their level of education, their experience, and their preparation and performance in the classroom. We still use the same criteria today. Our mentor teachers make the final decisions, but school principals and program heads provide input.

Mentor teachers receiving laptops

The bonuses we hand out have proven to be an excellent way to attract and retain high-quality teachers. Experience has taught us not to give the same amount of money to a teacher who is disinterested and uninvolved as we give to one who is creative and hardworking. Public schools in the U.S. should take note.

Despite the stipends and bonuses, in CFC's early years our teachers remained uninspired and underqualified. Most of them had only taken a six-month teaching course. We may not have had a single teacher who had graduated from college. Very few had the experience or training to teach the detailed, government-mandated curriculum in a way that was interesting to their students or themselves.

When CFC started training its teachers, it proved to be a game changer. Since 2006, volunteers from two schools in Singapore (the Singapore American School and the Tanglin Trust School) have been visiting Siem Reap two or three times each school year to conduct teacher training programs. In three-day workshops, Cambodian teachers are taught to set aside the traditional "chalk and talk" method of teaching in favor of one designed to engage students. Using games, experiments, and other creative strategies, the trainers show CFC teachers how to make the most challenging aspects of the subjects they teach come alive. Today we have four mentor teachers who observe classrooms and make specific suggestions on how teachers can improve their performance. They conduct weekly training sessions. More than anything else we've done, our teacher training program has revolutionized the country's education system.

The Cuong Do scholarship program

Food for Thought

As much time and effort as we spent training our teachers, we devoted a greater amount addressing the needs of our students. We noticed early on that many of them were arriving at school hungry. The piece of candy or bread given to them by a friend at lunchtime might be all they ate during the entire school day. Learning on an empty stomach is nearly impossible, and malnutrition was one of the leading causes of absenteeism and visits to the school nurse. If we wanted our children to participate in class and retain information, I knew we were going to have to provide them with nutritious meals. We started by serving an informal breakfast under a makeshift tin roof at our school in Spien Chrieve. We named the program Food for Thought. Almost instantly we could see a difference in the children who started their day this way. They looked healthier, had more energy, and were more interested in learning. It was clear to us that we needed to expand the program to our other schools as quickly as we could find the funds. Making that a priority, we soon had a cafeteria and a cook on each of our campuses. In February 2011 we were able to expand the program to include lunch.

Young student eating breakfast

Today, Food for Thought serves about 240,000 nutritious meals each month and nearly two million per year. Aptly named, the program is a large part of why CFC students are able to concentrate in the classroom, and why they attend school in the first place. For each meal, they stand in line with their bowls in hand and bow in gratitude to the volunteers who serve them. They then return to their tables, where they eat in almost total silence, treating the meal with quiet respect. When they're finished, they clean their bowls and utensils in the sink and brush their teeth. I can barely get my own children to do this at home, yet these kids do it happily and express genuine appreciation for the meals they receive. This mealtime ritual is a beautiful thing to observe, a stark contrast to the noise and clatter of school cafeterias in the U.S. Volunteers often tell me that their most memorable experience in Cambodia is serving CFC students a meal.

Going deep rather than wide offers so many rich rewards—seeing the empty breakfast bowls, knowing that the self-esteem of our girls will only continue to soar, and watching teachers mentoring their peers and then becoming mentors themselves. It works. It really works.

You can go deep not wide in your own life too. Make priorities and keep them. Family. Friends. Your bother, whatever that may be. You can't do everything, but you can do a lot. And "a lot" times many will change the world.

THREE

CHALLENGE YOURSELF TO STAY BOTHERED

Becoming bothered is easy. We're all bothered when we watch the news, see the homeless, or read about the refugee camps on the Arabian Peninsula. *Staying bothered* is much more difficult. There are going to be serious challenges along the way. Embrace them. Put solving them on the very top of your to-do list.

CFC didn't transition from a vague idea to the groundbreaking organization it is today without a few stumbles. In the early years we didn't know what we didn't know. *Everything* was a challenge, so we tried to avoid the word. *Challenge* was just another name for an opportunity to provide a better education for the children of Cambodia. When we saw that our adopted schools had problems, we made a commitment to do the best we could to improve them. Our mantra was "do more, talk less."

Kaye Bach, who played a crucial role in CFC's early success, liked to tease me by calling me "the lawnmower" because I would never stay still long enough to allow grass to grow beneath my feet. That was one of the key ingredients of our success. I always saw the next step we needed to take and pushed the organization in that direction. As soon as we had an elementary school up and running, we opened a junior high school. When our kindergartens were operating smoothly, we opened preschools. When we noticed the children were distracted because they were hungry, we began serving them breakfast and lunch. In April 2010 I looked at an open field in Aranh and imagined a high school there. A year later it was a reality. Former United Nations Ambassador Sichan Siv likes to remind me that his native country is a mess, but that CFC "looks at what is good and plows through the other stuff so it falls down around you."

Field where Aranh High School would be built

Fighting Bureaucracy

CFC operates government schools, which means we're required to follow guidelines instituted by Cambodia's Ministry of Education. When the Ministry issues a new rule that conflicts with our curriculum, which happens from time to time, it can create difficulties for us. For example, the Ministry recently decided to restrict computer classes to thirty minutes per day—at the same time it requires high school seniors to have forty hours of ICT (information and communication technology) instruction before they can graduate. Another Catch-22 is that the Ministry has made English mandatory, but not English *teachers*. We have to pay them ourselves.

The Ministry's directive that prevents teachers who stray from the standard curriculum from getting paid by the government has a direct impact on our operating budget. Anytime we ask teachers to deviate

CFC students in computer class

from the official curriculum—for our health, music, and Girls Matter! programs, for example—we're responsible for their salaries.

One conundrum we've begun to rectify is the Cambodian government's disinclination to pay our ICT teachers who don't have teaching certificates. Thanks to a scholarship program established by CFC board member Cuong Do, our ICT teachers have begun taking education classes at night at a local college or during the summer at the University of Phnom Penh. Furthering our teachers' education is extremely important to us. All CFC teachers have the opportunity to earn a university degree and study English, as long as they commit to teaching at a CFC school upon graduation.

Another challenge is that the government doesn't pay our preschool teachers, despite a federal mandate to create them. Our mentor teachers aren't paid by the government either, since they are our invention. Nevertheless, our mentors have proven to be crucial in improving the performance of our teachers. They are an integral part of the revolutionary model we're trying to promote.

Ours is a tiered system of teaching and training, which encourages the most experienced teachers to help newcomers. We want every teacher to become an agent of change within the Cambodian education system.

Another government mandate that produced a headache occurred in 2016, when thousands of contract teachers were hired and sent to schools throughout the country. The intent—solving the country's severe teacher shortage—was a good one, but the contract teachers were seriously underqualified. Most of them had graduated high school, but that's about it. The main reason they got the job was they were willing to work for almost no pay.

Just like that, we were handed thirty-five contract teachers and instructed to put them to work immediately. Our principals and teachers—and many parents, too—were outraged. Our teacher trainers in Singapore weren't happy either. We soon had a minor rebellion on our hands.

The CFC community was proud of how much the quality of teaching at our schools had improved, how we'd set the bar for what teaching in Cambodia could look like. Suddenly, however, our teachers' collective experience and skill level had plummeted. The contract teachers we'd been handed weren't even at the same level as our most inexperienced teachers. They couldn't attend our teacher training program because they wouldn't understand what they were being taught. Everyone with any stake in CFC came to me and said, "You have to do something."

I protested directly to the Minister of Education. "You can't do this to us," I told him. "We're the model schools for the entire country. We're what you want your education system to look like."

CFC operates government schools. Accepting contract teachers was one of their rules, and we had to follow the rules. We tend to forget that in much of Cambodia, particularly in the most rural areas, children are still showing up to classrooms without teachers. The Minister noted that his number-one problem, besides a lack of money, was finding teachers. "So here are some teachers," he told me.

A few days later I had a conference call with our leadership team in Siem Reap. "I'll tell you what we're going to do," I said. "We're going to make lemonade."

I asked students at Lehigh University in Pennsylvania to put together a paper outlining the ABCs of teaching. Our mentor teachers adapted it into a ten-week workshop aimed at improving the most basic teaching methods, including fundamentals such as how to present themselves, how to engage students, and how to effectively move from one classroom to another. Our message to the contract teachers was: "This is the way we do things here. We're going to support you with the tools necessary to do your job well."

We slowly eased the contract teachers into our fold, but on occasion we were forced to speed up the learning curve. When the government created a new rule requiring ESL instruction to start in the seventh grade, we had to scramble to get more English teachers. To fill the gap, we transferred many of our librarians, who tended to be our best English speakers, to the classroom to teach English, and we placed some of the contract teachers in the libraries. Our mentor teachers trained both groups.

The process was like playing musical chairs, but it worked. At the end of the school year, we gave every contract teacher a certificate signed by me and sealed with the CFC emblem. It may have only been a piece of paper, but to them it was a diploma. That paper, combined with the training we provided, energized most of them. For the first time in their lives, they felt good about themselves professionally.

Corruption

As it is in many countries, corruption is as ingrained in the Cambodian economy as the sale of rice. Like other countries where corruption is prevalent, the cost of nearly all goods and services is inflated by "padding," an informal tax placed on imports, construction work, deliveries—*everything*.

Perhaps because we're viewed as innocents in a den of thieves, CFC has largely been spared. Corruption always centers around an exchange—"I'll give you this as long as you give me that." But all CFC does is give. We never ask for anything in return.

Another advantage is that our funds go directly into our schools. Most NGOs, particularly larger ones, send their money through a government agency, and it gets doled out on the other side—after everyone has taken their little piece. We don't have that problem because we keep only ongoing expense money in Cambodia.

However, we're not immune to minor shakedowns. While CFC has tax-exempt status due to a memorandum of understanding with the government, our shipments sometimes get held up at the airport. Ung Savy, our country director, often urges me to pay the "import fee" and move on, but I'd rather have a dozen computers or a pallet of food sitting in storage at the airport for a week or two than pay an unauthorized tax. In the long run, that has worked, since local bureaucrats have learned they can't shake us down.

More troublesome to CFC has been minor corruption that has on occasion gained a foothold in some of our schools. A few years ago we were getting constant pushback from the teachers at our high school in Bakong about nearly everything we were trying to implement. The teachers were ignoring our most fundamental rule, that no student should have to pay to go to school. Many of them were demanding payment for private tutoring and, worse, charging students who wanted to improve their grades. The final straw was Savy's discovery that teachers were selling answers to the upcoming national exam.

Bill and I flew to Siem Reap for a sit-down with the principal and some of the teachers. We told them straight out that if they weren't going to follow our rules, we would seriously consider letting go of the school. We had done our best. We had placed Sivang, a "Camerican" (Cambodian-American), on the ground full-time at Bakong. Her job was to encourage the teachers to embrace our philosophy, strategies, and curriculum. But they were fighting her tooth and nail. At our other schools, most teachers embraced our Girls Matter! and Life Skills programs and jumped at the chance to participate in teacher training, but at Bakong High School we had trouble getting teachers to participate. We also learned that the school was "double-dipping"— taking money from another NGO for expenses and programs CFC was already funding.

It was no empty threat when I told them if they continued to disrespect us, we would pull out of the school. We could be tough because we were ready to make an example of Bakong. I had already cleared the idea with Savy, his team, and CFC's board of directors. Natalie Bastow and I were fully prepared to make the change. This was shortly after the EpiPen incident, so I was in full warrior mode, taking no prisoners.

The leadership at Bakong backed down. They knew that being part of CFC gave their school tremendous advantages. We still have a few problems there, but most of the teachers are now genuinely trying to work with us. Policies instituted by the new Minister of Education over the last few years have also helped. Cambodia has an end-of-the-year exam similar to the Regents Exams in New York and the STAAR Test in Texas. That exam is now kept under lock and key until the day it is administered, which prevents cheating. Test scores initially plummeted, but looked at with an eye to the future, it's been a positive development.

Government corruption has never been a big problem for us, but it did upset me when it occurred in our own backyard. It was important for us to take a stand. If we could show the kids in our schools and the people in the surrounding community what truth and honesty looked like, that was a big win for us.

Our no-nonsense response was part of a bigger lesson about staying bothered. It wasn't about revenge, which is a common reaction for people when they're bothered about something. Burning bridges wasn't going to help anyone in this situation. To stay bothered, we needed to stay calm, cool, and collected.

Campus Problems

Every CFC campus is now equipped with wireless internet, a breakthrough that cuts both ways. On the one hand, the internet is a fabulous teaching tool that has brought the outside world to communities that, prior to its existence, were extremely isolated. On the other hand, contact with the rest of the world exposes these communities to the sort of bad behavior only the internet can produce. We've had to train our teachers to moderate their use of social media. Until we put a stop to it, they were regularly posting pictures of themselves partying during the weekends, as well as posting inappropriate messages about their students.

Like every school in the world, ours have also had to deal with illegal drugs making their way onto our campuses. We have a zero-tolerance policy when it comes to students taking or selling drugs on school property, and on some of our campuses, we've had to fence off the most isolated areas to keep out uninvited guests.

At the same time, we also recognize that every "hoodlum," as Savy calls them, is not irredeemable. In their weekly meetings, our mentor teachers discuss with teachers why a particular student is doing poorly or is frequently absent. We're not trying to solve every child's problems, but when a CFC student expresses anxiety or depression, acts out in class, or repeatedly skips school, we schedule a home visit. What follows is a team effort. We might send a mentor teacher, a principal, a nurse, or a gender equity or life skills counselor to speak with the parents. Often Savy attends too.

With significantly fewer resources at their disposal, CFC schools in Siem Reap have better support systems than the public schools in Austin, Texas. During the 2016–17 academic year, our schools had 179 interventions, mostly for high absenteeism, but also failing grades, health issues, and violence at home. When we started to see an alarming jump in the dropout rate at Bakong Junior High, we took a deep dive into the numbers. As it turned out, a dozen girls were older than their records indicated and had been married during the school year.

As much as we try to help our students, we're not social workers. When students need assistance, we refer them to places better suited to addressing their needs. In Cambodia, most support groups aren't widely known because they tend to be run by foreign NGOs. To rectify this, we asked a Lehigh student to compile a list of places where families can turn to for help. We've made the list available to all our students and parents.

Empowering Communities

Staying bothered is life-changing, but effectively staying bothered requires the buy-in of the very people you want to help. "A hand up, not a hand out," has always been one of my mantras, and it was co-opted early on by CFC. Our schools are the models for the rest of the country because our communities have bought into our strategies; they are the ones who make it work. Our job is to empower principals, teachers, and students. Those who live nearby benefit as well, as they bring their buckets to the water filtration systems that provide safe drinking water on all our campuses. Likewise, the thousands of bicycles CFC has distributed since 2003 not only allow students to get to school, but also enable family members to look for work, shop in adjacent neighborhoods in search of better prices, and visit family and friends.

Distribution of bicycles to CFC students

Students bring home what they are taught at school, such as how teeth brushing, hand washing, and drinking clean water can positively influence a family's health. They also share with their families more complex lessons about disease prevention, nutrition, fitness, and reproductive health.

Getting parents involved is another practice we hope all Cambodian communities will emulate. Each semester, hundreds of parents and community members attend informational meetings about intestinal worms and parasites, dengue fever, and the importance of hygiene.

They participate in community meetings, where we distribute soap, toothpaste, and toothbrushes donated by corporations or other nonprofits or purchased through our own fundraising efforts. We've also established the first preschools in Cambodia. Because of the genocide that mars Cambodia's history, many new parents have no older female role models and, as a consequence, struggle to raise their children properly. CFC's twelve preschools have succeeded in educating not just small children, but entire families. In a country where healthcare is often inaccessible or unaffordable, we introduce new mothers to health and hygiene practices that many around the world take for granted.

CFC's water filtration systems serve students and their communities

Empowerment Saves Lives

The idea that empowering communities with knowledge can help save lives was brought home to us one Sunday afternoon. During one of our regular Monday calls, I asked Savy how his weekend had gone.

"Interesting," he said in his usual understated manner. "One of the preschool moms saved the life of a local child."

Savy explained how the lessons taught at a CFC preschool had paid huge dividends the day before, when a few local families were having a holiday picnic by a stream. As they were eating, someone noticed a small boy floating facedown in the water. A group of men pulled the boy out, turned him upside down, and, holding him by his ankles, began to shake him.

Fortunately, one of the mothers had been shown how to administer CPR by a preschool instructor, who had demonstrated on a doll. She recognized what the men were doing was perfectly wrong, and likely harmful. She grabbed the boy, laid him down on the ground, pumped his chest, and blew air into and out of his mouth. A few moments later, he started coughing up water.

Spien Chrieve villagers

The villagers who witnessed what the woman had done were beside themselves. They started talking at once, asking each other, "How did she know what to do? Where did she learn CPR?" That a woman had known how to respond when the men had not was an additional wake-up call.

Sometimes empowering members of the local community can have unintended consequences. Several years ago, Tong, a young man with a perpetual smile, began hanging around our schools, volunteering for every construction project or other task that was underway. Savy told me he was one of twelve children and was practically starving

Tong with Tom McCabe during a MAD trip

himself, using his entire salary to feed his family. At one point, he was so malnourished that he wound up in the hospital.

We ended up hiring Tong, but much to our surprise, he decided to become a Buddhist monk. Savy tried to talk him out of it, telling him he had a bright future working for CFC, but Tong insisted he was destined for a spiritual life. We were a little dismayed to be losing him, but also proud that we had been able to help him support his family and assist him in finding his true calling.

As satisfying as it has been to see CFC's influence spread from the school campuses into the local communities, we have to be careful to allow this to happen organically and not push our agenda onto others. To do otherwise would be to stray from our mission of educating children. Deep, not wide, remember?

Profound, meaningful, long-lasting change comes from focusing on one thing and doing it well. When people start to see the results of your hard work, it emboldens them to stop procrastinating and do something about what bothers them.

The Bridge

Not every venture I've attempted in Cambodia has been a success. A few years ago, I opened an art gallery near the Old Market in Siem Reap. Imagining it would provide a link between education and art, I named it The Bridge. I hoped it would appeal to tourists by making a clear distinction between what the gallery was selling and what could be purchased at one of the many outdoor markets in Siem Reap. We featured student art, as well as professional works, including jewelry designed by the Austin artist Kendra Scott. Any income the gallery produced would go straight into CFC's coffers.

Chris Churcher, chairman and president of CFC Singapore Board of Trustees who runs the Red Sea Gallery in Singapore, gave me some excellent advice, suggesting I should avoid having an artist run the gallery. In his opinion, creative minds were not wired for business.

It was without a doubt a great recommendation. I wholeheartedly agreed with it—then proceeded to ignore it.

Pen Rithy is a talented artist who also seemed to understand my vision for the gallery. I hired him to manage it, and I allowed him to display a few of his own pieces. In addition to a monthly salary, I had an apartment built for him in the back, where he lived for more than a year.

I had created a business plan I thought would work. It didn't. My vision was spot on; my execution much less so. You cannot run a business successfully if you don't regularly walk in the door. I had found a beautiful space, but my visits two or three times per year wasn't enough. I needed a better plan for managing and hiring employees. I had envisioned that the gallery would sponsor art classes and volunteer events, but I never found anyone on the ground in Siem Reap who shared that vision. In any venture like this, teamwork and partnering with like minds is critical. That's been a key to CFC's success, but it's also an explanation for why the gallery was not.

The Bridge art gallery in Siem Reap

In the end I had to assume responsibility for the failure. It was a learning experience. It reminded me that you can put all your energy into a project, but that doesn't guarantee success.

Seeing the art gallery fail hurt because I only had myself to blame. I had ignored Chris Churcher's advice, and I didn't delegate properly or efficiently. I went wide, not deep. The only consolation was knowing that setbacks, like the many other challenges CFC has faced over the years, can have a net-positive effect. They remind you to stay bothered about what matters.

If you never confront challenges, or failures, staying bothered is not possible. Setbacks still hurt, but they give you the wherewithal to plow ahead, and down an exciting new path. Try to let go of the failure. Move on and learn. Stay bothered smarter and wiser.

FOUR

WHEN LIGHTNING STRIKES YOUR HEART

One of my favorite singer-songwriters is Colbie Caillat. She has a song called "Brighter Than the Sun" that talks about how sometimes, in the blink of an eye, it feels like lightning has struck your heart.[1]

That's exactly what happened to me in the fall of 2004 when suddenly my bother became personal. Roughly a year after CFC got started, I met nine-year-old Rathana for the first time. She was by herself, playing with a few rocks in front of her school, which at the time consisted only of a small concrete building and a bamboo hut.[2] It must have been lunchtime, or perhaps school had just let out for the day, because other than Rathana, the campus was deserted. She later told me that ever since she had seen me distributing backpacks the year before, she had hoped I would notice her among the other children. Even at that young age, she was precocious.

While planning the construction of a new CFC building, I began to regularly visit Rathana's school, and she and I often spent time together. We quickly developed a bond. With Savy translating, Rathana told me stories from her life and from her imagination. I taught her some English, and she in turn explained what it was like as a child growing

---

[1] From "Brighter Than the Sun" by Colbie Caillat; https://www.youtube.com/watch?v=KU5o6M7S5nQ

[2] We would soon build our first CFC school on the site, the Amelio School, named after Bill's mother who had passed away earlier that year. Opening day was on her birthday, October 24.

Rathana and Cherry as young girls

up poor in post-Khmer Rouge Cambodia. Each time I returned home to Singapore, I couldn't get her out of my mind. It was almost as though she had cast a spell on me. She was, and still is, captivating.

One day Rathana invited me to meet her family. She lived with her mother, two brothers, and two younger sisters. Their house, like most homes in Spien Chrieve, was set high off the ground on stilts to protect it from the floods that come every year during rainy season. It was filled with the sound of the members of their large extended family constantly coming and going. Rathana's mother, Davy, introduced them to me as grandmothers, aunts, uncles, and cousins, but there were so many of them I couldn't keep all the relationships straight. It was only years afterwards that I realized I should have been paying closer attention.

After I'd been visiting Rathana for about a year, she introduced me to Cherry, a classmate who lived down the road. Rathana said they were best friends. *Opposites attract,* I thought to myself, because their personalities were very different.

Cherry was extremely shy, although underneath her sweet veneer was a steely determination. My earliest memories of her are of a barefoot young girl pedaling to school on a bicycle that was much too large for her. Watching her small legs furiously pumping, I should have been able to predict how brave and strong she would grow up to be. There was a lot going on during that time that I failed to see.

By this time, Rathana's father had another family. Neither of Rathana's parents was very engaged in raising their children. Her mother, in particular, had a contentious relationship with them. I never heard her say a kind word to Rathana, and when Rathana eventually came to live with us, Bill and I worried about her each time she returned to Siem Reap.

Cherry enjoyed a much more stable upbringing with her parents and older brother Niwat, who is currently studying to be a doctor. Her father, Savin, is a nurse, which makes him an important person in Spien Chrieve. A busy one, too—people from miles around think nothing of showing up at his door at all hours of the day or night in search

Three mothers: Davy, Bopha, and me

of medical attention. Cherry's mother, Bopha, took the interruptions calmly. As a small child, she had been forced by the Khmer Rouge to work in the fields seven days a week, so she took life's more ordinary events in stride. As an adult, her reaction to a lost childhood was a dedication to her family.

Rathana, Cherry, and I soon became a threesome, getting together each time I visited Siem Reap. With Savy as translator, we talked about what they were learning in school and their expectations for the future. These conversations fascinated me and provided a crucial window into the lives of our students and what they were imagining for themselves.

At this point, CFC was in full swing. We followed the opening of the Amelio School with the adoption of several other schools. Our initiatives, such as the Food for Thought program and the Teach-the-Teachers seminars, were changing lives. At the same time, my attachment to the children we were helping to educate and to the communities we were serving was growing stronger. I couldn't stop thinking about giving a Cambodian child a different kind of opportunity by coming to live with me and my family.

Rathana and Cherry in Singapore

In March 2005, when CFC sent a dance troupe from Siem Reap to the Singapore American School, the idea of opening our home to Rathana moved to the front of my mind. The three days the dancers spent in Singapore were life-changing for them. They had never been on an escalator before, much less an airplane. Rathana and her brother Pen Ratha, both members of the troupe, stayed in our home, along with three other girls. None of them spoke English, but they giggled the night away with Riley, Bronson, and, to the extent she could, baby Avery.

After the dance troupe's visit, I began talking privately with a few friends and CFC colleagues about the idea of bringing Cambodian children to Singapore for an extended stay. We imagined what it would mean for them and for our own families. We weren't considering formal adoptions, but we knew that for this to work, we'd need to become their legal guardians.

For one reason or another, everyone else lost interest in the idea, but I couldn't stop thinking about what the opportunity an extended stay in the U.S. would mean for a girl like Rathana. The health scare she suffered in April clinched it for me. She spent nine days in the hospital with a tooth abscess. Until the antibiotics kicked in, the left side of her face was paralyzed, and she remained in critical condition. In Singapore, I knew she would be healthy and safe.

There was just one small problem. I had become equally close to Cherry. Could I really invite one without the other? When I broke the news to Bill that I wanted two girls to come live with us, he was bemused but not surprised. As always, he was supportive. In our twenty-five years of marriage, Bill has, more or less, never denied me anything. He didn't this time either. In this case, however, my pitch didn't require much selling because Bill had also fallen in love with the children of Cambodia, specifically Rathana and Cherry. He has always been just as committed to CFC's success as I am.

At a full Amelio family meeting, the vote was unanimous: Rathana and Cherry would be coming to live with us—as long as their parents agreed.

With Savy as my interpreter, I explained to the girls' parents that we hoped to enroll them at the Singapore American School, where Riley and Bronson attended. I assured the parents that the girls would stay in regular contact through Skype and would visit home regularly during school vacations.

Cherry's parents were enthusiastic. The decision wasn't easy, particularly for Bopha, but she and Savin understood that Cherry would be given a unique chance to improve her life. Under the Khmer Rouge, Bopha had been forbidden to attend school, and she and Savin were committed to their children getting a good education. By the end of the conversation, they were in tears, sad to see their daughter leave, but happy she was being given such an extraordinary opportunity.

Rathana's parents viewed the idea on a more practical level. The move to Singapore would mean as much for them as for their daughter, as they would have one less mouth to feed.

After receiving each of the parents' blessings, I promised to care for the girls as if they were my own. I left their homes with a profound feeling that I had accomplished something incredible, but in my haste to get my plan approved, I had forgotten one of CFC's core tenets:

Bronson, Riley, Cherry, and Rathana in Singapore

deep, not wide. I had always done a good job of reminding myself to stay focused on our mission, but I had failed to carry that idea over to my personal life. I will never regret the decision to take in Rathana and Cherry, not even close. But by incorporating these girls into my family, I was going wide and, in the process, extending my emotional resources to the limit.

Fish Out of Water

My family and I welcomed Rathana and Cherry into our home with streamers and balloons. We put a big Welcome sign in the bedroom they would be sharing. Austin came home from college to be part of the celebration.

Because Rathana had visited with her dance troupe, she showed Cherry the ropes—from playing music and computer games, to bathing and flushing toilets. Cherry was particularly fascinated with the indoor plumbing, but in truth, everything was a learning experience, including meeting strangers, making friends, dining at restaurants, and watching the movie *High School Musical* over and over again (which helped them with their English more than any lesson plan ever could). We also were fortunate to have the wonderfully patient ESL (English as a Second Language) teacher at the Singapore American School work with them most days after school for two years.

Acclimating to the new environment wasn't easy. During the fall of 2005, they were in culture shock pretty much the entire semester. Homesickness was a real challenge for Cherry, while Rathana suffered from motion sickness every time she rode in a car. Both had difficulty learning English, and they dealt with persistent stomach issues from the abrupt changes in their diets.

In the Amelio household, tough love is usually accompanied by a warm hug and a lot of hand-holding. If Rathana or Cherry did something wrong, or if I was trying to encourage them to do better, I embraced them and said, "No matter what, I love you." This sort of touchy-feeliness is quite foreign to Cambodians, but after a while I think they "embraced" our hugging habit. Once the girls were able to communicate a little better, their confusion about almost everything began to dissipate. Sports helped, as Cherry loved softball and Rathana excelled at soccer.

In social situations, Rathana tended to overpower Cherry with her self-assuredness. She was a chameleon, able to move seamlessly from one challenge to the next without revealing anything about what she was thinking or feeling.

Cherry's feelings were more transparent, and she was easier to comfort with a hug. While she may have been be wary of jumping into new things, once she did, she fully committed. In that way, she was like a worker bee or "the little engine that could." When faced with the daunting task of reading a book in English, solving a difficult math problem, or writing an essay for history class, Cherry tried and tried until she could eventually do it on her own.

After living with us for a few years, she wrote a paper describing how her mother had been denied an education but had taught her to believe in herself. Cherry obviously had absorbed the lesson. "I would never give up," she wrote, "because I want my family to be proud of me. The people in Cambodia will think if this little girl can do it, they can too."

I was so proud of Cherry when I read that.

Disharmony

In January 2006, I thought we had reached a turning point with Rathana and Cherry when they returned to Singapore after spending Christmas break with their families in Cambodia. When I picked them up at the airport, I was so excited. "Here are my girls!" I shouted. I felt the same way I did when Bronson and Riley returned from summer camp, as though my kids were coming home. When they walked off the plane, I could tell by their faces they felt the same way.

That moment turned out to be the high point of Rathana and Cherry's time with us in Singapore. As their second year with us began, all wasn't well in the Amelio household. Bill was only home on weekends, so it fell to me to referee the growing disputes among the children. The most frequent offenders were Rathana and Riley, who—as the two eldest—were clearly vying to be "ruler of the roost."

For years—too many years, as it turned out—I assumed that disputes were simply part of a normal sibling rivalry. Rathana was thirteen, Cherry twelve, and Riley ten, so of course there would be squabbles.

I naively convinced myself that the children would grow out of their disagreements—that for a family of eight, the situation was perfectly normal. But the frequent arguments in our household put a damper on life in Singapore. This was not what I had anticipated when I was talking with Rathana and Cherry in Siem Reap two years earlier and dreaming about them becoming part of our family.

During the second year they lived with us, the situation with Rathana came into clearer focus when she and Cherry returned from Siem Reap after Christmas break. Rathana sat me and Bill down at the kitchen table and told us she was also speaking for Cherry. Cherry looked on in silence, later admitting that in those days, she felt she had to go along with anything Rathana said.

"We don't know if we want to live with you anymore," Rathana told us. She followed this up with two demands. First, "Riley has to go." He was mean to them, she explained. She couldn't tell us anything more specific beyond him telling Rathana she was late for school or demanding she move over on the sofa.

Riley has to go? I thought. *Are you kidding me? On what planet would I choose one child over another?*

I scratched my head and made a mental note to ask Riley what the heck was going on.

Rathana's second demand was that she and Cherry should no longer be obligated to go to church with us on Sundays.

Bill and I were taken aback, to say the least. Luckily, Bill took the lead before I said anything I regretted. I could not force myself to be even half as calm as he appeared. Bill had a lot of negotiating experience to rely on—although not much of it had been tested on a tween. He told Rathana we would consider what she was suggesting and discuss it further when he returned home the following weekend. Clearly, Bill and I had to discuss this in private.

As befits our personalities, I responded to the situation on an emotional level, while Bill adopted a level-headed approach to fixing a problem. His experience at the helm of multibillion-dollar corporations, where multiple problems arise every day, no doubt helped. Feeling angry and hurt, my initial reaction was that Rathana could go back to Cambodia if that's what she wanted. She, like Cherry, had been raised as a Buddhist, but she never conveyed to us that she wanted to practice her religion. When I told Savy we would be happy to keep hosting Cherry even if Rathana returned to Siem Reap, he told me there was no way Cherry's father would allow her to stay in Singapore without Rathana.

Bill's view was we had made a commitment to the girls, and we needed to do our best to ride out this crisis. Rathana, like all children, was likely testing how much power and control she possessed in this new life of hers. He projected the attitude "This too shall pass," and, at least outwardly, the confidence that it actually would.

The next weekend Bill and I sat down with the girls and delivered our verdict: if they wanted to continue staying with us, they needed to go to church with us on Sundays. By no means did they have to commit to Catholicism; we respected their upbringing and wanted them to feel free to believe whatever they wanted. They were welcome to study Buddhism if they wished, either on their own or in a temple in Singapore, but we made it clear that attending Mass together was an important part of our family life.

As for the issues with Riley, we told her we would continue to monitor the situation and make certain a typical sibling rivalry didn't turn into something worse.

In the end, this particular crisis blew over. The hard line Rathana had taken was a bluff. She was never planning to return to Cambodia, and that gave us the opportunity to reinforce loving but firm boundaries.

Nevertheless, the incident succeeded in leaving Bill and me feeling troubled. Had we done the right thing in taking the girls away from everything they had ever known and thrusting them into such a foreign environment? What were they really thinking—particularly Cherry, who was always so quiet? Did she share Rathana's complaints? Was Riley being any more difficult than a typical preteen boy? Was there something I was missing?

The incident made me realize how troubling Rathana's behavior had been for many months. She had been rude to me so many times that I lost count. I had blamed it on the difficulty of having to transition to a new, unfamiliar world, but now I wasn't so certain that was the root of the problem. Worse, I was no longer confident I knew how to help her in order to fix the situation.

As busy as our lives were, we quickly moved on from the incident, in denial about the clues popping up everywhere that hinted at an even greater problem.

The Speech

By the time we moved back to Austin in 2010, our family dynamics seemed to have mostly sorted themselves out. Rathana and Cherry had been with us for five years and were now in the same boat as the rest of us—struggling to acclimate to life in the United States. Speaking and writing English was no longer as big of an issue for the two girls, although they possessed varying degrees of proficiency. The rivalry between Rathana and Riley persisted, but it was masked by more pressing issues, such as making new friends and getting used to a new school. The situation hadn't really improved. We had all just become more adept at ignoring it.

There was one incident, however, that did give me pause. At the girls' school, a private Episcopal academy in Austin, each day began with chapel, and once a week a different student was asked to speak. Rathana came home from school one day and told us she was going to be speaking that Friday and asked if Bill and I would attend. We were traveling a lot at the time, but we assured her we'd be there. Since we had a lot of public speaking experience, Bill asked her if she wanted us to look at her speech.

"No, I've got it," she said.

Despite the tension that existed at home, Bill and I were feeling proud and optimistic when we arrived at the chapel. I was beaming when Rathana started to talk about her wonderful mother and how inspired she was by her. About three-quarters of the way into the speech, she said her mother once told her, "Be the river and keep flowing in whatever direction it takes you."

I had never said that to her, and suddenly I understood that she wasn't talking about me, but about her mother in Siem Reap, a woman who had never been particularly kind to her and certainly not inspirational. Rathana was painting a picture of her birth mother that had no basis in reality. The quote she attributed to her was false as well. Later I was able to identify its origin: a poem by Paulo Coelho, which Rathana had surely found on my bookshelf.

During her speech, Rathana said not one word about Bill or me or how her life had changed in any way since leaving Siem Reap. The rose-colored glasses I had been wearing exploded. If I could have dug a hole and buried myself in it, I would have, but I was in too much pain to do or say anything. I was hurt and embarrassed; all I could do was drag myself home and cry.

These difficult moments with Rathana made me distinctly uncomfortable. The only good that came from them was that they were healthy reminders of where my journey with these two little girls had begun. I had been bothered about their lives and wanted to improve them. I had used that discomfort as fuel. Seen in this light, being uncomfortable was a positive. I feel so strongly about the benefits of removing yourself from your comfort zone that it drives me to want to put others in that position. Maybe that explains why I was so interested in Rathana and Cherry coming to live with us, but it also worked the other way around. I often took Austin, Riley, Bronson, and Avery with me to Cambodia and other developing countries. The best advice you can give your children is the example you set. I want them to be bothered when they smell foul odors in the streets, see children who don't have the advantages they do, or hear about families seeking to sell their children. I don't want them returning to the U.S. and forgetting

Cherry and Rathana in Austin, 2014

about these experiences. I want the unfamiliar and the uncomfortable to stick with them and bother them, just as I want other people to be bothered, because that bother is the key to affecting real change and growing up to be a good person. We have repeatedly told our children almost from birth, "To whom much is given, much is expected" (Luke 12:48). As they grow into adults, my hope is that message will resonate. **A real bother is always personal, always passionate, and always forever.**

FIVE

———⟨∿⟩———

TAKE YOUR BOTHER WITH YOU

You can take your bother anywhere; it can pick up your spirits.

At least, that's what I thought when seven Amelios arrived back in Austin in June 2010 after a decade in Singapore. Our eldest, Austin, was already living downtown, attending community college.

"Home" is wherever your head hits the pillow. Everyone knows what you mean when you say, "Let's go home," whether it's after a night out, spending a long weekend at a hotel, or visiting a friend. But in my case, Texas really was home, which is why I thought repatriating from Singapore to the United States would be a piece of cake. Sure, I was leaving heaven on earth, where we had a great home, my kids attended an excellent school, and we were part of a tight-knit, expat community. But I was fortunate to be returning to something equally wonderful: a beautiful home on a lake in Austin, Texas, just an hour from where I grew up. After years of living abroad, I planned on living there forever, surrounded by my children and grandchildren. I should have been ecstatic about returning home, and I was—for about twenty-four hours. Then the "repatriation blues" set in.

Repatriating is never easy, and the fact no one prepares you for it only makes it more difficult. I wasn't ready for it at all. While countless books and articles are available about living abroad as an expatriate, there's very little information to prepare you for the equally disorienting shock of repatriating. Corporate America does a great job of preparing employees who will be living overseas for any length of time. The prescription for success is clearly laid out for them. Embrace the new culture. Be open to surprises. Treat everything as a learning experience. Be curious. Study a map. Learn about the healthcare system. Expect to be homesick. But no one tells you about repatriating, that "home" will not seem quite the same as it did when you left, that you will have changed, but invariably your friends and family will have not.

When I returned to Texas, I was bursting with excitement and tales of adventure and enchantment. My friends in Austin, however, weren't particularly interested in hearing my stories. They had barely heard of Cambodia, and almost no one could find it on a map. No one cared that I had once eaten tarantulas for dinner, scuba dived in Borneo, and explored Vietnam's Ha Long Bay by boat. I should have taken more seriously the advice of a friend who had repatriated from Singapore to the United States a few months earlier. "You'll be grateful just to be able to stand up," she had warned. Ha! That was never going to happen to me.

All seemed fine at first. Although our house on Lake Travis was sparsely furnished when we arrived, we felt comfortable living in a place where we had spent plenty of summers and Christmas vacations.

The first few weeks were chaotic and disorienting, but the kids seemed to be adjusting just fine. Wanting to keep them busy, I enrolled them in all sorts of summer activities. As the start of the school year approached, I insisted that fourteen-year-old Riley try out for football. He was an excellent athlete, and I was certain a team sport would help him adjust. He was reluctant, but I persisted. One day during the first week of practice, he called me. "Mom, I think I broke my hand." The emergency room doctor confirmed his diagnosis. So that didn't work out so well, but I was trying my best.

Our soon-to-be kindergartener, Avery, seemed to have the easiest time making the transition, ten-year-old Bronson the hardest. Every friend Bronson ever had was back in Singapore. Despite the football disaster, Riley was doing fine, as were the sixteen- and seventeen-year-old Cambodian girls we had made part of our family—particularly Rathana, who always seemed to go with the flow. Cherry, a year younger, quietly watched from the sidelines, waiting to see how everything was going to turn out. Their response to the situation matched their personalities. Rathana was confident. Cherry was reserved, and a little timid.

With Bill deep in negotiations for a new job, I was in many ways the odd person out. As our kids made new friends and did their best not to be viewed as different, I was left to figure out my life in this old/new environment.

Virginia

During our time abroad, Bill and I had known it was inevitable that we'd be returning to the U.S. one day. With this in mind, I had always found comfort in the fact that my best friend, Virginia, would be there waiting for me. With her at my side, adjusting would be easy.

Virginia and I had met decades earlier, in a very different incarnation of my life. My dad died when I was seventeen, and shortly after that my mother moved to England to care for her family. Barely into my twenties, with a baby and a difficult first marriage, I needed help, and Virginia was there to provide it. Eighteen years older, she became my mentor. She talked to me about marriage and what it meant to be a good mother, daughter, and friend. She gave me the courage to face divorce and single parenthood. I would not have survived those years without her support, and that bonded me to her for life. After I moved to the opposite side of the world, we still talked by phone almost daily. For more than two decades, she was the one constant in my life.

Virginia took her job as Riley's godmother seriously. When she came to North Carolina to see us a few days after he was born, she marched into the room and said, "Give me that baby," and started talking to him as if they had been friends forever. Years later, during spring break in 2010, Riley, Virginia, and I went out to dinner. Afterwards we said our good-byes in the parking lot—although Virginia and I never used those words. "I'm not saying good-bye," we'd say to each other, "because I'm always coming right back."

Virginia and Riley

Two days later, as soon as Riley and I landed in Singapore, I telephoned Virginia. She mentioned that she had a cold, but she said otherwise she was fine. That was Thursday. When we spoke on Saturday, she didn't sound right. Sunday, she answered her phone but said she would call me back.

She never did.

I repeatedly called her on Monday but got no answer. Tuesday night, her daughter, Amanda, called from the hospital and told me her mom had pneumonia and was in bad shape. I kept my phone with me every second until Amanda called again. She was crying and told me she needed me. I got on the next plane out. Traveling from Singapore to Austin takes about twenty-five hours. I arrived just before midnight on Wednesday and took a taxi straight to the hospital.

Virginia's friends spent the next few days praying, laughing, and hoping. We never left her side. On Good Friday I went to church, and on Easter Sunday I called Virginia's priest. He put oil on her head and together we prayed.

I felt an enormous responsibility to do exactly what Virginia would want me to do, including taking care of her daughter. I explained to Amanda what the doctor had made clear to me, that her mother didn't have much time left. Amanda went to Virginia's house and picked out a gorgeous cream silk dress, Virginia's best silk bedding, and her favorite scarves for us all to wear. Back at the hospital, we kissed Virginia and told her we loved her. This time it really was good-bye. All the machines except for the heart monitor were shut off. Seconds later it beeped. I looked at the nurse, who nodded his head.

"Amanda, honey," I said, "she's gone."

Virginia's death forced me to look at life without a filter. How do you go from talking to your best friend every day to suddenly knowing you'll never speak to her again? I still catch myself rehearsing in my mind all the things I want to tell her about my day. The service was held in Austin on April 9, which also happened to be the seventeenth anniversary of the day Bill and I were married.

Two months later, after my family and I had moved back to Texas, the sense of loss stirred in me all over again. Virginia had always guided me through the highs and lows of my life, whether it was falling in love with Bill, or dealing with our son Austin's troubles, or the difficulty of getting Caring for Cambodia on its feet. Rain or shine, she was always there for me.

I had done a pretty good job of blocking out the pain and confusion created by Virginia's passing, but when I returned to Texas, the hole she had left in my life threatened to swallow me. I nearly fell apart two months after returning from Singapore, the day the movers showed up with our furniture. What had I been thinking? They kept bringing more and more of our "stuff" into the house from a truck the length of a city block. I didn't need any of it. Why had I shipped easily replaceable furniture nine thousand miles from one house to another?

That question begat a slew of others. Why had we left paradise in the first place? With Bill once again traveling every week for work, how was I going to juggle the busy lives of six children by myself? And what about my "other children" now thousands of miles away, all the young Cambodians who deserved an education but couldn't afford one?

Virginia's death was difficult enough for me when I was living half a world away. Back in Austin, it was unbearable. As much pain as it caused me, however, I kept hearing her voice inside my head telling me I could get through this, too—that I *would* get through it.

Once the school year began, life became even more complicated. Most of my children's classmates had known each other since the first grade, many even earlier. The moms had formed nearly impenetrable adult cliques, which resulted in me feeling deeply isolated as I sat alone at my children's football, lacrosse, and volleyball games. My life had become a scene from *Big Little Lies*, but I didn't have Reese Witherspoon or Nicole Kidman to guide me.

With my children and my CFC colleagues, I never wanted to appear weak or beleaguered. I was their leader. I could handle everything on my crowded plate and then some. I was in control, and everything would be just fine.

But sometimes I felt overwhelmed, such as the time one of our important volunteers told me she wanted to resign. Like me, she was dealing with repatriation challenges. When she asked if I could start looking for a replacement, I broke down and cried. I'm always the tough one, telling everyone we will get past whatever obstacles were placed in our way. This time, I begged her to stay, and she did. CFC has succeeded because hundreds of people from all over the world, despite the challenges of their own busy lives, have made staying bothered a priority.

That friend wasn't the only colleague to share with me the difficulties of repatriation. Another, Liz King, warned me that one of the most difficult aspects about coming home was the disparity between how much she had changed and how much her old world had not. Marybeth Shay, who had been with me the first time we handed out backpacks at the Kravaan Primary School, was another friend who taught me a thing or two about the challenges of repatriation. She shared with me a mathematical formula that her international moving company had given her to calculate how long it should take her to acclimate: if it took six to twelve months to adjust to your host country, expect to double that before you can expect to successfully repatriate.

Marybeth likened the experience to trying to put a genie back in the bottle. What is this genie exactly? In my case, it had a lot to do with my ability to explore exotic new worlds. For a girl who grew up in Schertz, Texas, long weekends in Australia, Bali, Hong Kong, Thailand, Vietnam, and Cambodia—just to name some of the places my family and I visited while living in Singapore—opened my eyes to worlds I'd never dreamed existed. A decade in Southeast Asia introduced me to truly foreign smells, customs, and attitudes. The food, the people, and the natural beauty were enchanting and left an impression that will remain forever.

Then it suddenly stopped. The dream life was no more, as I was thrust back into a world far less exotic. Two hours by air from Singapore, there are dozens of incredibly beautiful and interesting places to visit. Two hours from Austin is . . . Kansas. (Not that there's anything wrong with Kansas.)

Two Full-Time Jobs

As difficult as it was for me to repatriate, I didn't have much free time to fret about it. I had two great responsibilities, both full-time jobs. While I was helping my children acclimate to their new environment, I was also learning on the fly how to operate CFC from an entirely new vantage point—eleven time zones away.

I realize now that when I told myself that moving CFC's headquarters to Austin would be seamless, I was in denial. I still spoke with CFC's deputy director, Ung Savy, nearly every day. I had met Savy in 2003 during one of my first "Orange Moments." A friend who had enlisted his services as a tour guide introduced us, and we quickly discovered we shared a common belief that Cambodian education could be vastly improved. Savy knew the lay of the land, and I was confident he could help our organization maneuver through the challenges we would inevitably face. Over the course of the next ten years, he and I built CFC one daily telephone conversation at a time. Simply put, CFC could never have experienced any of the success it has enjoyed over the years without him. Each time I spoke with him, his dedication encouraged me to renew my commitment to staying bothered. I'd hang up the phone and say to myself, "I can't let this guy down." Little did I know, he would soon let me down.

Early CFC photo of Savy and me

At least once a week I also talked to CFC's president, Natalie Bastow. A music teacher in Canada for a dozen years, she had moved to Singapore in 2006, when CFC was working hard to improve the skills of our teachers. After visiting our school in Bakong, she began devoting endless hours to CFC. She started as a member of our Education Committee, organizing a "Cut and Paste Club" that used colorful images pasted on large pieces of cardboard to illustrate Khmer stories translated into English. Over the years she took on more and more responsibility, and by the time I moved back to Austin, she was president, in charge of all our activities in Singapore, including our teacher training program. As much as anyone, she is responsible for CFC's growth and success, and leaving the organization in her tremendously capable hands made my return to the U.S. much easier than it otherwise would have been. I quickly settled into a routine of talking to Savy and Natalie during the early evening, which was conveniently their early morning. For the moment at least, we didn't skip a beat.

While CFC was running smoothly in Siem Reap and Singapore, operating it from Austin was a challenge. Suddenly I had lost my support system, as well as a major part of my identity. As CFC's "head cheerleader," I was often recognized in Singapore. Everywhere I went—school events, church fundraisers, even the grocery store—I was known as "that CFC woman." Strangers would bend my ear and I theirs about what we were doing in Siem Reap and what else needed to be done. I was constantly in recruiting mode, in search of volunteers, financial contributions, and new ideas about how to improve our schools. Uprooted from that environment and transplanted to the U.S., I felt I'd been separated from a part of myself.

Without CFC in my life 24/7, I was hit by the reality that there were other worlds beyond the education system in Cambodia. In this new environment, it was easy to become distracted. I had to constantly remind myself that I had made a lifelong commitment to CFC, and I needed to stay bothered.

Students and parents in Singapore raising money for CFC

At times, it was all too easy to get sidetracked. Fretting about what to do with all the furniture the moving company unloaded at our house in Austin stole days from my life. Pining over the loss of Virginia stole weeks. Even more distracting was the comfort of falling into old routines and living in a familiar culture. It would have been easy for me to get swept away by the tidal wave that is America, comforting myself with drive-through coffee shops, pizza deliveries, and the latest fitness craze. Almost daily I had to remind myself to stay bothered about the problems that still plagued the Cambodian education system nine thousand miles away. That's why staying bothered can be so difficult. When you move from one place to the next or from one job to another, your thinking often undergoes a change as well. What was critically important to you one day can lose nearly all its luster the next.

One memory has always helped me stay on track. The third time I visited Cambodia, I walked up to the window of a classroom and saw a little girl with a paper heart she had pinned to her shirt with a safety pin. "Jamie Amelio" was written on it in bright, clear letters. That sent a chill through me. "Uh-oh," I said to myself. "I'm in this now." Someone snapped a picture of that little girl and I've hung it in every office I've ever had, where it serves as a daily reminder to stay bothered.

The low point for me as a repatriate occurred when the headmaster of our children's school in Austin invited Bill and me to her home for dinner. I imagined telling her all about CFC and trying to establish a connection between our work in Cambodia and my children's school, just as we had done in Singapore and with Bill's alma mater, Lehigh University. Those arrangements had been a win-win for both institutions, as visiting the schools in Siem Reap had enriched SAS and Tanglin in Singapore and studying our success had worked its way into Lehigh's curriculum.

In Austin, I thought the headmaster had invited us to her home hoping to become friends and introduce us to other parents. I remember thinking the dinner might be the start of me feeling connected to the school and a way for me to become more involved in the community. Instead, during dessert she pulled out plans for a new building on campus, placed it on the table, and asked us for a large financial contribution. Bill and I were dumbfounded.

The next day I wrote to the headmaster describing our disappointment, but our relationship only worsened. When I met with the school's community service director, she told me they weren't interested in seeing another video of starving, dirty children. *Wow*. She was talking about CFC kids, *my* kids. This celebrated private school in Austin, which boasted of its commitment to "community and service," was just a wee bit hypocritical.

Apparently, in this new environment my affiliation with CFC was no longer seen as an accomplishment, but something of a limitation— if it was even recognized at all. That absence spawned what felt like an existential crisis in my life. If I wasn't "that CFC woman," who was I?

I felt rudderless. What helped me get through this difficult period and back on my feet was the very aspect of my life I'd been separated from: my hands-on, day-to-day connection to CFC.

I gained some much-needed confidence observing how another repatriate, my friend Liz King, had been able to maintain her commitment to CFC after she'd returned to the United States. Liz was part of the first wave of volunteers who turned Orange during CFC's early years. She was chair of our all-important Education Committee and was instrumental in the development of our teacher training program. With a master's degree in Education Psychology from UC Berkeley and extensive teaching experience, she brought a high level of expertise to everything CFC has done during the past sixteen years. When her husband was recalled to Washington, D.C., in 2008, Liz launched a new CFC chapter there. Staying connected to CFC, Liz later told me, became her way of avoiding the repatriation blues.

What worked for Liz ended up working for me after I observed her in action at a CFC board meeting in the fall of 2010. It was held at the Washington offices of the advertising firm Ogilvy & Mather. Years earlier, Ogilvy's global CEO, Chris Graves, had organized a team-building meeting in Siem Reap, an outing that had included painting a CFC school and building a playground. He had immediately turned Orange, and by 2010 both he and Liz had become board members.

Liz made the board meeting in D.C. special by reaching out to key members of the Cambodian-American community. When she called the Cambodian temple in Silver Spring, Maryland, to introduce herself and ask for advice, by a stroke of good fortune, Narin Seng Jamison answered the phone. Narin—Liz and I soon discovered—is the point person for almost everything Cambodian in the United States. She left Cambodia just before the Khmer Rouge took control of the country and committed herself to keeping Cambodian traditions alive in the U.S. That included resuscitating a culinary culture that had been all but wiped out. When I first met her, she had recently finished writing *Cooking the Cambodian Way: The Intertwined Story of Cooking and Culture in Cambodia*. CFC subsequently published thousands of copies and resold them one by one through various fundraising efforts.

At Narin's suggestion, we invited other notable Cambodian-Americans to the cocktail party that followed the board meeting. They included Hem Heng, the Cambodian ambassador to the United States from 2008 to 2015, and Sichan Siv, the U.S. ambassador to the United Nations Economic and Social Council from 2001 to 2006. As I would come to learn, Sichan's entire family had been killed during Pol Pot's reign of terror.[3] In his book, *Golden Bones*, he wrote about his "journey from hell in Cambodia to a new life in America." The title is a reference to a Khmer proverb that describes someone born very lucky, or very blessed.

Maybe it was the colorfully outfitted Cambodian performers dancing to Cambodian music juxtaposed against the U.S. Capitol Building in

---

[3] Pol Pot was the General Secretary of the Communist Party of Kampuchea (the Khmer Rouge) from 1963 to 1981.

the background, but during the event in D.C. I suddenly felt a surge of confidence that I could successfully transfer the leadership of our organization and our fundraising efforts to America. Maybe it wouldn't happen exactly the way I had hoped, but I saw that it was possible, and I knew everything was going to be okay.

As it turned out, my hunch was correct. Shortly after the D.C. event, Narin and Sichan introduced me to key members of the Cambodian-American community in Texas, kicking off a new chapter in CFC's history.

Channy and Savy

Two of the central figures in Austin's Cambodian-American community are Channy Soeur and Savy Buoy. Both of them, by their mere presence in my life, constantly remind me to stay bothered about Cambodia. Channy and Savy, strangers at the time, both fled Cambodia on April 17, 1975, one day after the Cambodian New Year and a day before the Khmer Rouge entered Phnom Penh and took control of the country.

Channy Soeur and Savy Buoy at CFC fundraiser in Austin

They were part of a group of seven hundred people, most of whom had been members of the Cambodian Navy, who fled Cambodia by commandeering three small naval ships.

Their arrival in the Philippines placed nineteen-year-old Channy and sixteen-year-old Savy on an immigration track to the United States. Thanks to an act of Congress, they were among the roughly 130,000 refugees from South Vietnam, Laos, and Cambodia who were allowed to enter the U.S. and given financial assistance.

By July 1975, Channy was living at a refugee center at Fort Indiantown Gap, a U.S. Army base in Pennsylvania. From there, a community organization relocated him to Providence, Rhode Island. During the next five years, he took on various menial jobs to support himself. Channy remembers "crying his eyeballs out" after standing on his feet washing dishes twelve hours a day. He only knew three words in English: "yes," "no," and "okay." Publicly, he claims to have learned the language at the library and trade school. Privately, he'll confess that his best English lessons came from American girlfriends, who he and his fellow refugees called "long-haired dictionaries."

Channy's dream was to study petroleum engineering, and in his estimation, the best place to do that was the University of Texas. After selling nearly all his possessions, including his car, furniture, and refrigerator, he arrived in Austin in 1980 with five hundred dollars. He slept on another refugee's couch until he was accepted at UT. Four years later he graduated with a BS in petroleum engineering and was hired as a draftsman for the City of Austin. In 1996 he was named assistant director of Solid Waste Services, becoming Austin's first Asian-American city executive. Five years later he started his own company, CAS Consulting & Services, which now has offices in seven cities. Channy also helped create the Austin Asian Chamber of Commerce, the Asian American Resource Center (AARC), and the Network of Asian American Organizations, and he has served as board chair of the Texas Federation of Asian American Chamber of Commerce.

Like Channy, Savy's life had been irrevocably changed in 1975. During the same stop in the Philippines, she and her seventeen-year-old sister were separated from the rest of their family. Their parents and siblings were sent to a refugee camp at the border of Thailand and Malaysia. Conditions were so bad that they were eventually sent back to Cambodia, where all of them, except for one of Savy's brothers, died of starvation.

Savy and her sister, however, traveled from the Philippines to Camp Pendleton in Southern California, where a refugee camp had been set up for Cambodians, South Vietnamese, and Laotians fleeing their war-torn countries. On July 4, 1975, Savy was sponsored by a family in Houston. Suddenly enrolled in the tenth grade, she remembers clutching textbooks she had no hope of reading and crying herself to sleep at night. Fortunately, the abrupt life change she experienced the following year was of a more enjoyable kind: she married a former Cambodian naval officer. They raised a family together in San Antonio. When I met her in 2010, she had begun a successful real estate practice in Houston and was volunteering at a number of Asian-American organizations.

More Than Colleagues

I first met Channy at the suggestion of Narin Seng Jamison and Sichan Siv. At a party at our home in Austin, we immediately recognized our different perspectives on Cambodia, but in a funny way that brought us together. More than three decades earlier, on the Cambodian naval ship heading toward the Philippines, Channy had vowed to himself that if he managed to survive the ordeal, he would never again have anything to do with Cambodia. Subsisting on rice and salt and feeling as though he had no country and no future, he had contemplated suicide. That was surely the low point in his life.

Nevertheless, we immediately hit it off. Channy made it clear that he still harbored negative feelings about his birth country. He considered the current Cambodian regime to be as corrupt, and nearly as brutal, as the Khmer Rouge who had murdered virtually every member of his family. He told me we had very different priorities. His was to improve the lives of Asian-Americans who lived in the U.S. He couldn't care less, he said, about anyone living in Cambodia.

"I will never go back," Channy said to me on more than one occasion. "You have your priority," he told me. "I have mine."

I considered that a challenge and told him I was going to convince him to reconsider. His stubbornness was just another lynchpin in my motivation to stay bothered.

One of the first things Channy and I accomplished together was to make Austin and Siem Reap Friendship Cities, the first step toward becoming Sister Cities. To speed the process, we invited the mayor of

Austin mayor Steve Adler at CFC school with his wife, Diane Land, Alex Tan, and Savy Buoy

Siem Reap to visit Austin, and two years later Austin's mayor, Steve Adler, reciprocated, joining Channy, Savy, and me on a trip to Cambodia.

Channy's trips with me were difficult for him, partly because of the promise he had made to himself more than forty years earlier. He continues to disdain the corruption, leniency toward human trafficking, and disrespect for the law that he believes still defines the country of his birth. Nevertheless, Channy has met me halfway, and I don't think he has ever regretted his trips to Cambodia with me.

Savy Buoy has also accompanied me on several trips to Siem Reap and has helped organize every CFC fundraising event in Austin. While she shares Channy's frustrations with Cambodia, she has become an invaluable member of CFC. Helping children in Siem Reap attend school is particularly meaningful to her since not all that long ago, she was one of those children.

Ironically, Channy and Savy have been able to accomplish a great deal for the Cambodian-American community in Texas, while the most significant achievements I've made have taken place in Cambodia. Savy and I often joke that she or Channy would make a great mayor of Austin, while I would be an effective mayor of Siem Reap. Both of them have become more than colleagues; they are friends who have inspired me in ways they probably don't imagine. During difficult times, when I've thought that there was no way I could continue to run CFC from halfway around the world, I reflect upon their lives and remember how much they've been through and how much they've accomplished. When I do that, it's not so hard to stay bothered.

Bamboo Strength

As much as my Cambodian-American friends in Austin and my passion for CFC helped me get out of my repatriation funk, I have to give myself a little credit too. You must take care of yourself before you can take care of others. When I'm in the car alone, sometimes it's just a matter of turning up the music really loud. **Music helps me feel the thoughts I may not**

know I have. It's no wonder Bon Jovi's "Who Says You Can't Go Home"[4] became included in my playlist. I felt as if that song was written for me, a hometown girl searching for where she belonged.

During my most challenging times, I have also relied on another coping mechanism, which might not be the best remedy for everyone but works wonders for me. I head straight for the nearest tattoo parlor!

I acquired my first tattoo in 2001 as a response to the loss of identity I was feeling in Singapore. During my time there, I was expected to assume a variety of roles: wife, mother, friend, nonprofit executive, and Texas expat, to name several. With so many social responsibilities I was expected to fulfill, I sometimes stopped to ask myself, "Where is Jamie?"

One Saturday morning I told Bill I was going to the grocery store. Instead, I stopped at a local tattoo parlor and began looking through hundreds of photos. I settled on the Polynesian sign for Sagittarius. Not only was it gorgeous, but I thought Bill might be "less mad" if he knew I'd been thinking about him. He's a Sagittarius, and we had gone to Polynesia for our honeymoon.

I spent the next six hours being poked with a needle, most of that time regretting my decision. I felt even more sheepish years later when I learned I'd gotten a "tramp stamp"—though no one was calling it that at the time.

Bill's reaction was a predictable "What the—?" Eventually he came around, as he would with all my subsequent tattoos. He's come to understand that each of them was a response to a difficult time in my life, my way of dealing with external pressures beyond my control. It's one of the many reasons my love for Bill runs so deep. I'm a wild child compared to him, but while he might not be overjoyed about my tattoos, he assures me that it's my body and I should feel free to do whatever I want to it. Through all the chaos and challenges that regularly come my

---

4 From "Who Says You Can't Go Home" by Bon Jovi, Jennifer Nettles https://www.youtube.com/watch?v=5CeX5VEo10c.

way, Bill has always supported me full throttle. Without that support, I think I would have gone off the deep end long ago.

I got my second tattoo the day after Virginia's funeral. Following the service on April 9, 2010, we released butterflies into the air as a sign of resurrection, but also as a way to lighten our hearts. Afterwards her daughter Amanda, Austin, and I got identical butterfly tattoos. To a certain extent it helped us feel better. We had no choice but to laugh when we realized that the more color there is in a tattoo, the more pain is involved, and we'd chosen one of the most colorful creatures on the planet!

In early 2013 I returned to the tattoo parlor. This time, however, I wanted to *reflect* the strength I was feeling, not *find* the strength I lacked. The design of this tattoo was also much more elaborate.

For some time, I had wanted to cover the right side of my body with stalks of bamboo. In Cambodia, like so many other places in Asia, bamboo grows wild and is extremely prolific. It's an amazing plant. It bends but does not break. It's relatively thin, but thanks to its deep roots, it is incredibly strong. It also bounces back easily, even after every part of it that's above ground has been destroyed.

Bamboo is very useful too. It can serve as an excellent windbreak from gale-force storms. A bamboo grove is considered one of the safest places you can be during an earthquake—because the roots are so deep and wide, the ground won't split open. Bamboo can also be used as a building material, a fiber, a fuel, even a food source. You can eat the plant's shoots and they will replenish themselves the very next day! In other words, bamboo is a perfect example of flexibility, resilience, strength, and sustenance. With a bamboo tattoo, I was hoping to capture and project "bamboo strength." Even during the most difficult times, I wanted to be able to look at my own body and remind myself, "I can do this!"

My bamboo tattoo continues to grow, just like me. I keep returning to my preferred artist, who bears a striking resemblance to Harry Connick Jr., so he can add more stalks, more color, more life. There's something about the needles entering your body, injecting the permanent ink under your skin, that makes you focus on the here and now. But boy, it is painful.

I don't look like the type of person who would have a full-body tattoo, and I like that aspect of it too. Once while I was driving Avery and her friends home from school, they started playing the game Two Truths and a Lie. When it was Avery's turn, she said, "I met Justin Bieber, I almost got hit by a kangaroo, and I dyed my hair blonde." I'd once let Avery highlight her hair, and she was almost hit by a kangaroo while we were vacationing in Australia, so the lie was meeting the Biebs.

The kids begged me to take a turn, so I told them, "I have sixteen tattoos, I've swum with sharks, and I've climbed Mt. Everest." They guessed the lie was that I have sixteen tattoos, but if you consider each stalk to be an individual tattoo, I have at least that many. I swam with sharks in Langkawi, Malaysia, in 2008, but I'm never going to climb Mt. Everest.

My two most recent tats are the only ones visible when I'm dressed professionally. In early 2015, after the previous year had been particularly tough, I decided I wanted something that screamed power, so I had the Khmer word for "strength" tattooed on my right forearm. Now when I meet with government officials or construction workers in Cambodia, they know I mean business.

On my other arm, I have a tattoo of a lotus flower. From muddy waters blooms a flower that retreats at night, but by noon the following day, it is once again bright, strong, and beautiful. It symbolizes inner strength, persistence and, ultimately, success. To me, that's what staying bothered is all about. "Fearlessness is fearlessness" became my mantra. I didn't know then how much that conviction would be tested.

SIX

DECEPTION, BETRAYAL, FORGIVENESS

Sometimes staying bothered takes a powerful hit. When that happens, and it will, you have to steel yourself against deception and negativity, pushing through to the other side with fortitude and forgiveness. That's what I had to do during the summer of 2013 when I learned that every person I trusted most in Cambodia had been lying to me every day for ten years.

I should have become suspicious when, just after school let out for the year in 2013, Rathana and Cherry told me, *on the same day,* that their grandmothers were ill and their families needed money to pay for a doctor. As if that weren't a glaring enough clue, Chok Dary, Rathana's aunt and the principal at the Amelio School, told me just around the same time that *her* mother was sick, and she asked if she could take a few days off. Still, I thought it was all just a coincidence.

A few weeks later, July 24, 2013, started innocently enough. Bronson and Riley spent the day at camp. Avery, Cherry, and I were relaxing by the pool. Rathana was in Siem Reap for the summer. She was living with Savy and his wife, Mum, but Bill and I talked to her regularly by phone.

In March Rathana had been offered a partial scholarship to the prestigious School of Visual Art and Design at the University of South Carolina. I had urged her to attend, explaining what a tremendous opportunity it was, but she told me she didn't want to live in the South. Obsessed with the *Twilight* series, which takes place in Washington State, she was hoping to attend school in Seattle.

Bill and I suggested she take a gap year in Cambodia, after which we could resume our discussions about college. We were absolutely ready to pay for her continued schooling, but we thought she could use a break to return to her roots, work on herself, learn to be grateful, give back, and serve others.

When Rathana called to tell us her grandmother had died, I immediately relayed the news to Cherry. She seemed upset, but it was difficult to gauge the depth of her emotions because she kept running upstairs to her room. When she told me she didn't feel well, I assumed she was jet-lagged. She had just returned from Cambodia to get ready to go to college in San Antonio.

Later that night I was in my office answering emails when a sudden "ping" from my computer told me I had received a new message—from Cherry, who was only one floor away. I had to read her note twice before what she was telling me fully sank in. Addressed to Bill and me, it laid out a pattern of deception that had been initiated years before by Savy in Cambodia. "This is what I want to tell you," she wrote. "Rathana and I are cousins. Everyone is related. Mum is Rathana's oldest sister, so Savy is Rathana's brother-in-law. We're all related."

I couldn't believe what she was telling me. Her grandmother, Rathana's grandmother, and Chok Dary's mother were all the same person! I read the email a third time. I was stunned, but I recovered enough to run upstairs, lie down on the bed with Cherry, and tell her I loved her.

"You don't hate me?" she asked, tears streaming down her face. "You can send me back."

I put my arms around her and said, "No, I don't hate you. I love you. You know that."

Cherry told me the decision to reveal the deception had been torturing her for many weeks, and her parents, particularly her father, had been urging her to finally tell me the truth. Now that Cherry's grandmother had died, Savin thought it was absurd to keep the truth buried any longer.

Cherry was a mess, and her distress made me cry too. I wanted her to know everything would be fine, that nothing had changed between us. I didn't blame her. She and Rathana were young children when they were first told to perpetuate this lie—this oh-so-unnecessary lie—by every authority figure in their lives.

Cherry was just a month away from starting her first year at college. She'd already gone through orientation and was preparing to move into her dorm room. Now she was convinced that part of her life was over. I assured her that the way Bill and I felt about her hadn't changed and of course she'd still be going to college.

Cherry was blameless, but I was furious at everyone else as I began to finally connect the dots. *Everyone* was in on the deception. All the most important Cambodians working for CFC on the ground in Siem Reap were, much to my surprise, related. Rathana's mother, Davy, was the sister of Cherry's father, Savin. Savy's wife, Mum, was Rathana's half-sister. Rathana and Cherry weren't "best friends"—they were first cousins.

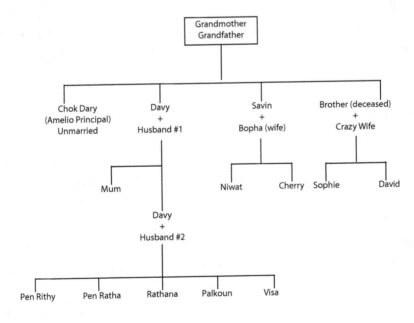

Family tree explained

I forwarded Cherry's email to Bill and sobbed on the phone while he comforted me. I was much more upset than he was. He mostly felt bad for me.

Savy's betrayal hurt me the most. Our relationship had always been so solid—or at least that's what I thought. I wrote a blistering email to him but, heeding Bill's advice, I waited until the weekend before doing anything.

My friends and the CFC board members were sympathetic, but none of them really understood my reaction. Looking at the situation from thirty thousand feet, what was the big deal? Their attitude—understandably, I suppose—was, "Why are you so upset? Because the girls are *cousins*?" They didn't understand how it felt to realize that every Cambodian I had trusted had been deceiving me every day for nearly a decade.

Confronting the Truth

In Cherry's email, she begged me not to tell Savy that I knew the truth. I didn't want to betray Cherry's trust, but my hesitation only delayed the inevitable. I don't think Cherry had given a lot of thought to what would happen after she emailed me. She had been focused solely on finally unburdening herself. I explained to her that sooner or later, the lie would have to be exposed.

A few days later, unable to hold off any longer, I fired off an email to Savy that was only slightly toned down from my original draft. I told him how angry, humiliated, and betrayed I felt. I was upset, and I didn't hold much back.

When Bill returned on Friday evening, he immediately did the same thing I had. He went to Cherry's room and told her we loved her unconditionally and understood how difficult it must have been for her to keep this big, complicated lie to herself all these years. Ever since she was ten years old, Cherry had seen her world continually turned upside down. She had faced challenge after challenge as she transitioned to life in a foreign country—and all the while she had to keep this silly secret. When Cherry sent that email to me, she was finally able to shed some of that burden.

In between sobs, Cherry also described a side of Rathana I had suspected but never fully seen. According to Cherry, Rathana had been bullying her for years. Insisting that she maintain the lie was just a small part of it. Rathana often belittled her and ostracized her at school. When Rathana had friends to the house, she wouldn't let Cherry join them, insisting that her cousin go to their bedroom to study. Now I was not only feeling brokenhearted, but guilty as well.

The lie may not have constituted serious criminal behavior, but with so many people asking for money for the same dying person, it did feel like a low-stakes swindle. In the spring, Chok Dary had asked me for an extra $150 to help pay for her sick mother's medical bills, Rathana had asked for fifty dollars to send to her grandmother, and I had given Davy fifty dollars to help her sick mother. Unbeknownst to me, over the years I had given *thousands* of dollars—all to the same person!

The sums may have been small, but I couldn't help feeling I'd been played. I began thinking of other times "the grandmother story" or something similar had been used. During the next few months I carefully reviewed CFC's financial ledgers. Fortunately I didn't find any other discrepancies. As skeptical as I had become about Savy's honesty, he has never given me any reason to doubt him when it comes to how CFC's money is spent.

After the truth finally came to light, I thought about the many instances when Rathana's and Cherry's extended family could have—should have!—ended the deception. The day I asked permission to take the girls to Singapore had been the most obvious opportunity. I wouldn't have cared; I would have simply chalked it up to a misunderstanding. They could have just blamed the language barrier and stopped the obfuscation in its tracks. Sure, I would have been surprised, but I certainly wouldn't have been devastated like I was years later. If they had just come clean with me from the outset, absolutely nothing would have changed. Bill and I still would have brought both girls to Singapore with us.

Instead, at least a dozen family members had continued to lie to me—at first by omission, then by commission. I was devastated because I had felt so connected to them. I had spent many, many hours in their homes. I felt like part of their family. I held their babies, ate their rice, met their grandmothers. But the entire time they were lying to me, even if it was about a very small thing. It felt as though they had continually been saying behind my back, "Joke's on her."

Once I knew the truth, I asked myself if I had missed any clues. Of course I had! There had been numerous times when I should have figured out what was going on, either by asking the right questions, or simply opening my eyes. How could I not have known?

I think the lie was difficult for me to see because it was so unnecessary. Would it have made any difference knowing that Rathana and Cherry were first cousins rather than best friends? Of course not. But as small as the lie was, it made me wonder if there was something else, something bigger they might be hiding from me as well. Perpetuating the lie didn't make any sense to me, but maybe it made sense to them. After all, this family was only a few decades removed from the brutality of the Khmer Rouge, a time in the country's history that was so horrific it normalized fear and mistrust.

Confrontation

I scheduled a visit to Siem Reap to confront the conspirators face-to-face. Bill didn't want me to go alone. There was lot at stake. CFC had dramatically improved their lives. If I were to force them out, it would put their livelihood and position in the community in jeopardy.

Savy had the most to lose. If I fired him, he would lose face with the Ministry of Education and would likely never find a comparable job. Savy is a gentle soul who, despite this large hiccup, had been my trusted partner. But still, you never know.

On the plane to Cambodia, I was feeling a lot of inner turmoil. I kept telling myself, "I have to let go; I have to forgive." That was much easier said than done. I needed to look them in the eye first. Only then would I know which part of me would win the battle tearing up my insides: my emotions, which were screaming at me to pull up stakes and run away, or my faith, which was advising me to forgive. I felt like I was in a cartoon, with the devil on one shoulder and an angel on the other. One moment I would think, *Why should I continue to be involved in a country where the people I trusted most have been lying to me?* The next moment, I would consider what the schools would look like in a year or two if I abandoned CFC. I'd say to myself, "I can't let this one incident destroy everything we've built."

Taking Bill's advice, I asked the relevant people to meet me in a public place, the Raffles Hotel in downtown Siem Reap. Rathana's mother was conspicuously absent, I suppose because she knew I would place much of the blame on her. Chok Dary also declined the invitation. When I saw her at the Amelio School a few days later, she acted like nothing had happened. But Savy, Mum, Rathana, Rathana's sisters Palkoon and Visa, and her brothers Pen Ratha and Pen Rithy were all there. I didn't mince words. I told them the deception they had maintained was the worst thing anyone had ever done to me, I was taking it personally, and I didn't know if I could forgive them. They were mortified and extremely apologetic. They seemed truly sorry, but I wanted some answers. I asked them who had orchestrated the deception, but they stonewalled.

After initially thinking Savy was mostly to blame since he and I were so close, I came to believe that Mum had been the orchestrator. That realization hurt me to my core. I had treated her like a little sister. I'm sure she would agree that my influence and business advice helped her become successful in real estate and grow as a human being. What's more, toward the end of 2011, when she and Savy were having difficulty getting pregnant, Bill and I paid for in vitro fertilization treatments.

After their son Dawson was born in July 2012, I wrote Mum a list of dos and don'ts on how to care for an infant. For years she kept it posted on her refrigerator door.

Savy, Dawson, and Mum

Savy made excuses for Mum, telling me she had never fully recovered from her own broken home. After she married Savy, her parents and extended family pushed her even further away.

I wasn't buying it. I asked them over and over again why they had perpetuated the lie. Why, why, why, why? But they didn't have an answer. It wasn't that they didn't have a *good* answer; they didn't have *any* answer. At one point, Savy did say they were worried that if I thought Rathana and Cherry were related, I wouldn't take both of them. That made no sense, yet it was all they had. They kept returning to Mum's difficult childhood as an explanation, but to me, that explanation seemed wobbly at best. "I don't care about her damn childhood!" I said at one point. "I'm your friend! You don't lie to your friends!"

I continued to dig for a reasonable explanation, but in the end, I had to accept that one simply did not exist. I had entered the meeting at the Raffles angry, but afterwards I was just sad.

Before returning to Austin, I took everyone on a boat ride in an attempt to resurrect the good feelings that had so recently existed between me and Rathana's and Cherry's extended family. Just outside of Siem Reap is a "water jungle," a floating forest of oversized plants jutting out of shallow, muddy water. We floated on small flat barges, hoping the coolness in the air combined with the stillness of the water would have a calming effect on the tensions of the past several days. After the uncomfortable confrontation at the Raffles, the trip was meant to be restorative. Instead, it made me wonder if my relationship with these people I loved and trusted would ever be the same.

Me on the boat, in the water jungle

Forgiveness

Out of everyone involved, Savy showed his emotions the least. There was no way he would ever cry in front of me, but I could see in his eyes how much pain he was feeling. In retrospect, I'm convinced that keeping his feelings bottled up inside is what made him sick.

Savy didn't look particularly well that day at the Raffles, and each time I visited Siem Reap over the course of the next twelve months, he looked even worse. Mum regularly called me in a panic with updates about his declining health—first to say he had lost feeling in his hand, then to tell me that his vision had grown blurry. When he started losing feeling in his feet, he had to stop driving. Some days he was so weak he could barely walk. We sent him to multiple doctors and hospitals, but no one could figure out what was wrong with him.

CFC's other top people and I kept Savy's illness to ourselves. I didn't want to think about the possibility of losing him, but Bill, Natalie, and I were eventually forced to consider it. Savy supervises our entire operation on the ground in Siem Reap. He is our intermediary with the Ministry of Education, and in charge of distributing all the funds and materials we collect. No single Cambodian could effectively replace him.

Despite seeing specialists at various medical centers, including an international hospital in Thailand, Savy's health continued to deteriorate. In May 2014, CFC sent him to a leadership program at Lehigh University. While there, he got a complete physical at the local hospital. Different specialists produced different diagnoses. One said he had nerve damage; another thought he had PTSD from his experiences in the Vietnamese Army. Another physician suggested his ailment was psychosomatic. The only consensus was that he should start taking vitamins and blood pressure medication.

Just before Christmas 2014, Mum called me in the middle of the night. "Savy can't get out of bed," she said. "He can't even open his eyes." The next day I flew him to Singapore. He stayed at the home of a CFC volunteer, Christy Machulsky, while he underwent a battery of tests at the

International Medical Clinic, which has partnered with CFC on several projects. Finally we got some answers. A few months earlier, doctors at a hospital in Bangkok had diagnosed him with a hyperthyroid condition, but they had prescribed medication for *hypo*thyroidism. These were two very different ailments. Taking the wrong medication had exacerbated his symptoms and was slowly killing him.

Savy and me when he was not well

Savy is now fully healthy. He even jogs some mornings. The health of our relationship has also been restored . . . for the most part. I still haven't fully recovered from the fact that he lied to me for so many years, although the more I spend time with him, the more our relationship resembles the way it used to be. We've always been a great team.

The first few months after the reveal were difficult, however. On certain days I came close to throwing up my hands and walking away. Then I would think about what the country would look like without the good work our organization did. I thought about what I would say to our volunteers and to the many Cambodian students I had gotten to know at our schools. What kind of message would an abrupt exit send? I didn't want to be guilty of stereotypically American behavior—intervening in the affairs of a foreign country, paying more attention to bricks and mortar than hearts and minds, and then walking away. In the end, I had to do one thing. I had to practice what I preached. I had to stay bothered.

Nevertheless, for many months I harbored negative thoughts. How could I run CFC, an organization based largely on others trusting me, when I no longer trusted them? I knew that if I was going to continue to work there, I needed to let go of my hard feelings and forgive those who had bruised them. Looking at it from a narrow point of view, I was mad at Savy, Mum, Davy, and Chok Dary, but if I pulled out of CFC, I would also be punishing the innocent children of Cambodia, their teachers, and the volunteers who devoted so much of their time and energy to the organization. Was I really going to abandon everything we had worked so hard to build because of my hurt feelings? I knew I couldn't shut down an organization that had done so much good simply because a few people had pulled the wool over my eyes. I kept telling myself, "I can't abandon this project. I need to stay bothered."

Once I decided that CFC must continue, I felt infinitely lighter, as if the weight of an elephant had been lifted off my shoulders. I came to understand how you can hold on to a grudge so tightly and for so long that it destroys you from the inside. I realized that forgiveness is not an emotion, but an act of will. I didn't *feel* forgiving, yet I still forgave them. I leaned on my Catholic faith. If I couldn't forgive others, how did I expect Jesus to forgive me?

Forgiving the families in Siem Reap allowed me to get moving again, to be the lawnmower that doesn't allow the grass to grow too high. While the experience bothered me, it wasn't the type of bother to which I wanted to devote my time and energy.

The rift among Rathana's and Cherry's family in Siem Reap has not healed nearly as well. Instead of blaming themselves for whatever role

Savin and Bopha, Cherry's parents

they played in the charade, they blamed each other. The two sides of the family are now estranged, picking and choosing which weddings and funerals to attend so they can avoid each other. When it was discovered that Cherry had been the one who had finally revealed the truth, her parents were ostracized from the rest of their extended family. Her father, Savin, had been CFC's full-time nurse for almost a decade, but after the deception was revealed, he felt that he could no longer work with Savy, and he resigned.

So what do you do with all this? In life, in business, in communities, in families, "stuff" happens. Your task during tough times is to find something, anything, that is good. Build on that. Focus on it every day. And keep going.

Me at work in Siem Reap

PHOTOS

Young Avery and me in Texas and a recent photo of us at Angkor Wat in 2018

Angkor Wat

C classroom BEFORE and AFTER

Bill and me with faculty and staff at Spien Chrieve School in 2002 and 2016

CFC female students – Girls Matter!

CFC Teachers: me with a contract teacher receiving her certificate; teachers and staff; teacher training; primary school teacher

CFC students eating lunch, Food for Thought Program

CFC students on bicycles purchased through donations

...udents' Collage: HS Student Council meeting; CFC health screening; CFC preschoolers; HS science fair

Riley in front of Arahn Primary School before it was renovated by CFC; CFC's Arahn MS; Riley and me in front of Arahn HS being constructed

Young Rathana (far right) with traditional Cambodian dancers performing at the first CFC school opening

Rathana (left) and Cherry (right) alone and with Bill and me; and with the Amelio family (Cherry, Riley, Avery, Rathana, Bronson, me, Austin and Bill)

Austin as a teenager with my BFF, Virginia

My bamboo tattoo

My arm tattoo, which says STRENGTH in the Khmer language

My Texas "Framily" (l-r) Pete Barolotta, Rick Flores, Bill, Hope Bartolotta, Joy Bartolotta, Bronson, Gary Whorton, Carol Whorton, and Pierce Bartolotta who really helped me out of my repatriation funk

My TedTalk Presentation about CFC and Being Bothered in 2014

Savy and me mulling over new ideas for CFC schools around 2015

Emcee Austin and me at CFC fundraiser in Austin

CFC Robotics Team at US Capitol competing in an international students competition in 2017

CFC high school graduates in 2017

Bill, Savy and me in 2002 and 2018

CFC Team Dee Gallo, HR Director Lori Soenkson, Accounting Director Lydia Breckon, Director of Development, me and Natalie Bastow COO in 2018

Cherry in Texas, 2018

Avery and me with Cherry's parents in Siem Reap, 2018

Avery with cousins and friends and me in Siem Reap, 2018

Bill and me at Riley's graduation, 2018

Bronson through the years

The Amelio guys travel to New Orleans for their beloved Steelers in 2018!

My coming to peace about the deception at a Cambodian mountaintop temple in 2019

Savy and me in step at Angkor Wat, 2019

Savy, me, and Samedi, 2019

Our grandson, Lev

The most recent Amelio family photo, 2019

This little girl has a nametag with my name on her heart.

SEVEN

———◁◁◁▷▷▷———

END GAME

Measure your successes, and reward yourself by feeling good.

I am truly humbled by what CFC has accomplished, and I'm so thankful to the thousands of volunteers who have assisted us and to the Cambodian communities that have come to understand the value of a quality education. If CFC has helped one child learn when they otherwise would not have had the opportunity, we have succeeded, and the many individuals who have helped us should feel proud.

It's easy to focus on our biggest accomplishments—building four dozen new buildings, creating new preschools and high schools, training teachers, and establishing Food for Thought. In 2017 the Cambodian government reaffirmed that CFC schools are the model for the rest of the country. That's a tremendous honor, and so is the fact that two of our teachers from Aranh were recently asked to help write the national exams.

On the ground in Siem Reap, however, it's the little things that have made the biggest impact on our students and their families. Here's a small sample of what CFC has done—sixteen achievements in the first sixteen years:

1. No more classrooms without a teacher

2. Ten-year-old girls being taught Girls Matter!

3. Textbooks telling the truth—even about the atrocities committed by the Khmer Rouge

4. Art classes allowing young children to paint or draw from their imagination

5. Music rooms offering a wide array of instruments, including pianos

6. Graduates returning to CFC schools as teachers

7. Women learning to be mothers in Cambodia's first preschools

8. A new pair of glasses that changes a child's entire perspective

9. Teachers displaying a desire to teach, and acquiring the necessary knowledge

10. World-class (clean) classrooms that provide a hospitable environment for students to learn

11. Dozens of children riding to school on their bicycles

12. Local families visiting our campuses to fill buckets with filtered water

13. A local fundraiser raising fifty dollars for the upkeep of a playground

14. CFC graduates starting businesses and working at local schools, restaurants, shops, and health clinics

15. Thousands of smiles displaying happiness, gratitude—and very clean teeth

16. Having CFC graduates come back to teach at our schools!

That's sixteen, but we could have easily listed sixteen hundred. During our time in Cambodia we've made promises, and we've kept them. In the process, we've changed a country—one school, one classroom, one student at a time. Now we've begun to look forward. How do we make the successes we've enjoyed permanent? How do we make certain that our communities, both in Cambodia and around the world, stay bothered?

Our first preschool, before and after

Sustainability

With decades of experience leading multibillion-dollar companies, Bill has taught me a lot about how to run a large organization, including the importance of focusing on the end game. In CFC's case, that means making the organization sustainable and scalable.

With Bill's influence, embedded into my philosophy of staying bothered is the idea of thinking long-term. Nothing is more frustrating than knowing that the changes you've worked so hard to bring about will disappear if you ever weaken your intense commitment to the cause. For the first decade of CFC's existence, sustainability was at the forefront of every move we made, and for good reason. It's what makes real change possible.

The key to making your organization sustainable, I soon discovered, is putting programs in place that will ensure its future even if you're not there to oversee them. The best recent example is Vegetables for Change, a program we launched in 2015 that fits well into our long-term strategy. It gives local entrepreneurs the skills and resources to build vegetable gardens on our campuses. Students and their families contribute some of the food they harvest to our in-school meals. They sell the rest at local markets.

After successfully injecting best practices into the Cambodian educational system, our hope at CFC is that Cambodians will grab the baton and run with it. That's always been an essential ingredient of our end game: establishing high standards in a handful of Cambodian schools and hoping those standards will permeate the rest of the country's education system, then phasing ourselves out.

We're working hard to make CFC sustainable, so that after Bill and I are long gone, CFC will continue to be a beacon for quality education in Cambodia. With this in mind, everything has been on the table at our CFC board meetings—even the idea of privatizing our schools and charging tuition. Sixty-seven hundred students paying a dollar or two every month would cover a lot of salaries. But then we started asking ourselves questions for which we had no satisfactory answers. Who would collect the cash and keep track of it? What would we do about students who were unable to pay? Would we continue to use the government curriculum, or would we need to develop our own? And the most damning question: wouldn't privatization contradict our mission to make higher education an attainable choice for all?

In the end, we decided that charging students is probably not the best way to accomplish our mission. At the same time, to be sustainable in the long run, we must figure out a way to eliminate our need for constant fundraising.

At nearly $150,000 per year, Food for Thought is CFC's most expensive program (and according to students and parents, our most valued). Part of our end-game strategy is focused on mitigating that cost. In 2014 a substantial portion of the Food for Thought budget was covered by fourteen-year-old Dylan Pallodino, who helped raise $125,000 for CFC by climbing Mount Kilimanjaro with his mother in an initiative called "Feeding Minds, Fighting Hunger." An in-kind contribution of $60,000 worth of fortified rice and vegetables from the Minnesota-based nonprofit, Feed My Starving Children (FMSC), has also been a tremendous help. We need to memorialize these contributions and implement cost-saving strategies in other areas. For example, while we will continue to give bonuses to our best teachers, we're hoping to gradually discontinue the stipends we give to all of them.

Last year, FMSC asked if we would become its Cambodian distributor. It was a tempting offer, but ultimately we decided to turn it down. As admirable as feeding every person in Cambodia is, it's outside our purview. As I've said, we are constantly wary of succumbing to charity drift, wandering into areas unrelated to our central objective of educating Cambodian children.

Building an Endowment

A successful end game will have to include ramping up our fundraising efforts to create an endowment that can offer CFC long-term, self-perpetuating support. For sixteen years, CFC has had success with fundraising aimed mostly at individuals. Thanks to our chief operating officer, Natalie Bastow, all donors, whether they give fifty dollars or $100,000, receive a handwritten acknowledgment. Single contributions have funded everything from a kindergarten teacher's annual salary to replacing an aging building at Bakong Primary and outfitting a music room with a piano and a dozen guitars.

Unfortunately, this sort of fundraising is unsustainable. The nonprofit organizations that stick around and make a lasting impact are the ones that receive consistent corporate funding. The method of fundraising we rely on—receiving the bulk of our budget from private donors—results in smaller contributions. It is exciting to have so many people personally invested in CFC, but it is much more difficult to maintain than large annual corporate or foundation support. We end up working

CFC students in the Bartolotta science lab

a lot harder for smaller amounts of money. This strategy needs to evolve.

Our goal is not only to use an endowment to keep our schools operating smoothly, but also to transition the decision-making process to local control. In the future, a Cambodian board of directors, not a group of Westerners in Singapore or Austin, will decide when a school's roof needs to be replaced or whether a new IT teacher should be hired. We will evolve from an organization that makes decisions from afar to one that is run by Cambodians making decisions about Cambodians, in Cambodia. For this to work, local involvement is essential. They are the ones who need to stay bothered. Fortunately, we began empowering parents and local communities long ago. Our computer and science labs and life skills courses are already under local control.

The support of Cambodian volunteers has helped tremendously. Parents donate their time and energy to CFC schools. When our libraries need new books, playgrounds need to be repaired, or classrooms need to be painted, local fundraising and physical labor has made a huge difference. Businesses in Siem Reap use donation boxes to raise funds. Recently, more than one hundred CFC supporters turned the Angkor Wat Half Marathon into a fundraiser.

Currently we have a two-pronged strategy. At the same time we expect to cut our operating budget in half within five years, we hope a bulked-up endowment will pay for the rest in the not-too-distant future.

Scalable

CFC has already shown its ability to be scalable, as government schools across the country have adopted many aspects of our curriculum. For example, the Cambodian Ministry of Education now requires and supports the kind of health programs CFC has been offering for years. We can also take partial credit for the Ministry's recent decision to mandate ESL beginning in the fourth grade rather than the seventh. CFC has long advocated that, in today's global economy, it is critical for Cambodian students to begin learning English as early as possible. CFC's ESL classes actually begin in the second grade, and some of our students start learning English in kindergarten.

Changes in Phnom Penh have helped. While most government-

ESL taught by the fabulous Sinat

run schools in Cambodia do not have dedicated English teachers, the government has recently started paying ours. This prevents the sort of corruption that occurs in other schools, where English teachers often make up for not getting paid by insisting on being compensated for "private tutoring." This kind of exploitation does not occur at CFC schools.

Another way CFC is proving to be scalable is our ability to monetize our all-important teacher training program. After a decade, our training has become valuable intellectual property, and we've started to share our model and techniques with teachers outside of CFC schools. Teachers from all over Cambodia now pay to attend our teacher training sessions. That's another important step toward self-sufficiency. Our trainers already receive honorariums for speaking at conferences. Recently, one hundred non-CFC teachers, including six Cambodian Ministry of Education employees, paid to attend one of our three-day training programs. The six are now teacher trainers themselves. Last year, CFC's two-day conference on ESL (sponsored by the MoneyGram Foundation) was attended by educators from every part of Cambodia. It focused on technology integration, student-centered learning, and other classroom management techniques. A few months later at CamTESOL, an annual conference in Phnom Penh attended by teachers from more than thirty countries, CFC's ESL staff shared their experiences teaching English to primary grade students.

An unexpected bonus of training non-CFC teachers is that when they return to their government schools, they share what they learned with their colleagues. At a recent off-site training, I asked a group of teachers from rural communities what they wanted most. In the past, the most common response was more money, a smartphone, or a new motorbike. This time, the majority said they wanted to become better teachers. That's a *huge* change.

Ideally, we'll create a teaching certificate program of our own that is officially recognized by the government in Phnom Penh. That would provide us with a steady inflow of paid, qualified teachers.

When I consider whether the model schools CFC has created can be replicated throughout the country, I remain hopeful, thanks in no small measure to the thousands of CFC graduates who have passed through our system. In 2016, 367 students graduated from our schools, including seventy-five who had attended them from kindergarten through the twelfth grade. In 2017, another 307 students graduated and entered the workforce.

We're proud of these numbers. According to data compiled by Lehigh University, our graduation rates are the highest in Cambodia. In 2016, CFC students earned a pass rate of 82 percent, compared to the national average of 62 percent. Similarly, our dropout rates are currently between 2 and 3 percent, far below the national average, which is well into the double digits. Our teacher turnover rate is also significantly lower than at other Cambodian schools.

We have high hopes for our graduates, who are part of a generation not directly traumatized by the genocide their grandparents were forced to endure. They are also benefitting from having been taught twenty-first-century skills—not only ESL, but also the sciences and computing technology. They've spent time in CFC classrooms that integrate hard and soft abilities—academic content and technical prowess. Critical thinking, creative problem solving, and new knowledge generation are in great demand in Southeast Asia's emerging economies, and that's exactly what we're teaching our students. Forty of our most recent graduates were awarded state scholarships, and four received interest-free loans from the Oasis of Hope Foundation to study at the University of Cambodia.

We're hoping CFC graduates will develop a community of their own. To speed that process, we're working to improve our alumni tracking program, although it isn't easy. Young Cambodians have cell phones, but they replace their SIM cards—and therefore their phone numbers—nearly as often as they change their underwear. Inviting every CFC graduate to join the Facebook page we created has helped, and we've started to organize class reunions.

We've given our Cambodian communities the tools to become self-sufficient; now it's time for them to take over. As much as I look forward to that day, I also realize exactly what it means: someone will be taking my job. I view the prospect of that happening with mixed feelings. I'm sad that a chapter in my life will be closing, but I'm overjoyed by all we've accomplished and all CFC will continue to achieve in the future.

EIGHT

BE OPEN TO A NEW BOTHER

Sometimes life throws you unexpected curves, and quite suddenly you're walking down an unfamiliar road. Your choice will be to retreat or move forward.

During the summer of 2016, our sixteen-year-old son Bronson was getting ready for his junior year at Lake Travis High School in Austin. He has dealt with medical issues his entire life. Born with a broken shoulder, as an infant he suffered from craniosynostosis, a premature fusion of the sutures in the skull. If left untreated, it can cause a multitude of problems later in life.

During Bronson's first few months, he wore a helmet that helped alleviate the pressure on his skull. A newborn grows fast, so doctors had to adjust the helmet frequently. Twice a week for six months, Bronson and I made the three-hour round trip from our home in Palos Verdes, California, to Burbank.

In the second grade, Bronson suffered another serious medical issue when he collided with a classmate on the playground. The teachers ran to help the little girl, leaving Bronson to walk alone to the nurse's office with a broken jaw and blood all over his shirt and hands. When I rushed him to the hospital, some of his teeth were poking through his lip. It broke my heart to see my little boy in a hospital bed with his jaw wired shut. Worse, his jawbone didn't heal properly, leaving him for years afterwards looking slightly different than his classmates. At least it was slight to me. At an age when kids want nothing more than to fit in, it didn't help that as a high school freshman, he began to wear braces.

The plan always had been for Bronson to have surgery to correct the shape of his jaw when he became a teenager and was more fully grown. The doctors warned us that otherwise his jaw would always be slightly off-center, he would be prone to headaches, and his teeth would likely not remain straight. In July 2016, after we tried to keep our minds off the impending hospital stay by spending two weeks in Cambodia working at various CFC schools, Bronson had the surgery.

Bill and I were a little naïve about the ramifications of what felt like a simple decision. Bronson had had a similar procedure when he was ten, and the recovery was relatively easy. Milkshakes for an entire month hadn't seemed much of a price to pay.

This time his jaw had to be broken, and the ensuing recovery was much more difficult. We expected Bronson would be back on his feet by the time school started. Instead, he spent the first several weeks of the semester still in pain. With his jaw locked, he could barely talk, and he was unable to eat anything solid. Three months passed before he could chew food without discomfort.

No one anticipated how emotionally traumatic the recovery would be. Beyond the constant pain, he was mortified by his appearance. He told us he looked like the Fat Bastard character in the Austin Powers movies, and he insisted that he didn't want to return to school. There was nothing I could say to convince him otherwise. I felt horrible—and helpless.

Even though he eventually did return to school, Bronson never returned to normal—whatever "normal" is—and he began to deal with his distress in ways he couldn't articulate. Making a bad situation worse, no one at school picked up on it. Not one teacher, counselor, or coach noticed how down in the dumps Bronson was, even after he began to self-medicate with pot.

The first few times I caught Bronson smoking, I chalked it up to normal teenage behavior. But then his grades began to decline, and he started calling me from school in the middle of the day, begging me to take him home. "I can't walk into class," he'd tell me. "I can't do it."

I would have to talk him down from the ledge. "You can do it. It's going to be okay."

Sometimes I gave in and picked him up from school, but his anxiety followed him home. Doing homework, the numbing paralysis returned. Those were the good days. On the bad ones, he would speak to Bill and me in ways he never had, lashing out as if we were the cause of his distress. Particularly when Bill was out of town, I tried to remain calm and repeat to myself something I recently had heard: "Remember that a problem child is a child with problems."

A young Bronson on skateboard

Bronson's behavior quickly began to snowball, however. All the classic signs were there: self-medicating, skipping school, getting grades that were unprecedented for him. He started getting high in his room and sneaking out at night.

As Bronson's spirits plummeted, Bill and I did everything we could think of to help. We disciplined him by grounding him and taking away one gadget after another, including his beloved skateboard. We spoke with his teachers, but they didn't offer much support, basically admitting they weren't equipped to handle this kind of problem. We sent him to a therapist. If he couldn't open up to us about what was going on inside his head, surely he could benefit from being honest with someone else. But no, Bronson told us we were wasting our money. Nothing helped.

In the spring of 2017, several incidents exacerbated Bronson's stress level. As a freshman, he had played varsity lacrosse. He was already six feet tall and a terrific athlete. Because of the surgery, as a sophomore he couldn't play fall ball. Just putting on his lacrosse helmet was painful, but the coach assured him he'd have a spot on the team in the spring.

Bronson was crushed when he showed up to practice one day and the coach pulled him aside and told him he was being demoted to junior varsity. Looking at it objectively, I understood the decision. Bronson was still dealing with the pain and a kind of PTSD from the surgery. He was not playing to his potential. His growing anxiety had begun to show itself on the field, sometimes leaving him frozen in one spot. Getting high all the time certainly didn't help his game either.

Nevertheless, as Bronson's mother, I was furious at the coach for the way he handled the situation. A coach is supposed to motivate and inspire, but the way he delivered the news to Bronson was cruel. He acted like the demotion was no big deal and expressed no concern at all about what Bronson was thinking or feeling. Not once did he ask Bronson what was wrong when, clearly, something wasn't right. The coach later apologized, but by that point the damage had been done.

Bronson playing lacrosse

Bronson experienced another setback one day after school when Debby, my Texas friend who is as close to my kids as any aunt, drove him to our old house to pick up his wakeskate.[5] We had moved from our home on Lake Travis to a new house just a few miles away. Our old house was for sale and nearly empty.

The front door was locked, so they walked around to the back, where they noticed that the door leading to the exercise room was ajar. When they stepped inside, they saw a backpack on the kitchen counter and a group of kids walking down the stairs. The room reeked of liquor and pot, and the place was trashed.

"What the hell are you doing in my house?" Bronson yelled.

He was beside himself. That morning, he had texted a few friends because they were absent from chemistry class. One of them texted back to say he was at home, sick. In fact, the kid was at our old house partying with Bronson's other "friends." It turned out these same boys had been sneaking into our empty house for weeks. Now, on top of everything else, he wasn't sure who his real friends were.

---

[5] A wakeskate is like a skateboard, but used on the water.

A security camera caught everything, so identifying the boys was easy. We pressed charges; Bronson didn't escape the incident unscathed, so why should they?

Lessons from Austin

In November, during one of his increasingly common rants, Bronson mentioned suicide. That was a red flag. No, not a red flag—a giant flashing neon billboard. Bill was out of town, but we were constantly talking by phone. I was at my wit's end. I considered calling 911, but instead I put Bronson on the phone with the woman Bill and I call our life coach. We've known Diane since 1998, and over the years she's helped Bill and me through our rockiest times, including my near-death experience. Bronson told her the same thing he'd been telling me, that if he couldn't have his skateboard, he didn't want to live.

That was the final straw. With Bronson growing increasingly anxious and depressed and now talking about suicide, we had rapidly approached crisis mode. Bronson had grown increasingly depressed, and it became clear to Bill and me that we weren't equipped to handle the situation on our own. I didn't want to repeat the mistakes I had made with our eldest son, Austin, who as a teenager had battled an addiction to alcohol. Austin has now been in recovery for more than a decade and is a successful actor with a five-year-old son. But during his high school years in Singapore, he was partying too hard and blacking out almost every night. He hit bottom one Sunday morning when he woke up on top of the ten-foot-high fence that surrounded our property. Trying to climb over the wall, he passed out on top. Bill and I agreed we needed to do something drastic to help him. We decided on a surprise intervention, followed by a stint at a rehab center in Dahlonega, Georgia. It was meant as a wake-up call—he was escorted onto the plane by two very large former policemen.

After Austin spent seven weeks in rehab, we made the mistake of allowing him to return to his old environment. Despite his assurances that he had changed, he fell back into his old habits almost immediately.

It wasn't until Austin spent a few months in Cambodia that, by the grace of God, he finally began to turn his life around. He spent many long days in the hot sun working for CFC, building schools, painting classrooms, and repairing playgrounds. Being thrown into a foreign environment with few of the luxuries he had always taken for granted was a turning point for him. "Cambodia saved my life," he said in an interview years later. "Finally, it was occurring to me that perhaps it's not all about me. Working in Cambodia made me look at my life from a bird's-eye view, almost like I was in the clouds looking down at my life in the States and seeing everything from a very different perspective. I asked myself, 'What the hell am I doing?' All these people here are struggling to feed and clothe their families. They go to the bathroom in the water where they bathe and swim. Meanwhile, what am I doing with my life?"

Bronson in Utah

With our experience with Austin clearly in mind, Bill and I told Bronson we were sending him to a wilderness therapy program in Utah. Remembering how Austin had responded so well to his time in Cambodia, we hoped a similarly rugged, remote environment would do the same for our youngest son.

Bronson wasn't happy about it, but Bill was firm. "The choice is yours," he told him. "You can either go willingly, or we'll have someone take you away forcibly."

Knowing that his older brother had, in Bronson's words, "got gooned," he believed us and complied. He spent the next eight weeks undergoing "wilderness adventure therapy" with an organization called Aspiro, backpacking in the Utah mountains, pitching his own tent, and cooking his own food.

Living in the wilderness, away from the distractions of the "real world," can be therapeutic. It pushes teens to be independent and think about life in a different way. The experience requires more from them than simply having to live without a cell phone. Hiking, cooking, and sleeping outdoors miles from civilization forces them to consider their place in the world and lends some perspective to the issues that might be troubling them at home. Those were the aspirations Bill and I had for Bronson. In the short term, we were just glad to know he was safe and being looked after by a group of highly trained professionals.

As much hope as we harbored, we knew the wilderness experience alone would not be enough; we knew Bronson wasn't going to simply come home and be free of the stress and anxiety he had been feeling just a few weeks earlier. Hoping not to repeat the same mistake we had made with Austin, we didn't want Bronson to come home until he was healthy. His therapist at Aspiro recommended a boarding school that would continue to give him the support he needed and the tools to deal with anxiety and stress. That's how Bronson ended up at the Telos Academy in Orem, Utah.

Telos comes from the Greek word for "purpose" or "goal," although Barry Fell, the school's executive director, defines it as "potential." That's a better translation because Telos is all about helping students reach their potential—as opposed to someone else's expectations of their potential. The school was founded sixteen years ago by a team of mental health professionals who wanted to develop a more effective treatment program for troubled teens.

In September 2017, Bill, Bronson, and I drove from Aspiro to Telos, stopping at a McDonald's along the way. After eight weeks of rice and beans, Bronson gorged himself on multiple cheeseburgers, fries, and milkshakes. As disgusting as the display was, it was gratifying to see him enthusiastic about something—even if it was stuffing his face with junk food.

During the drive to Telos, Bronson kept telling us that he was okay, that what we were doing was unnecessary. Bill and I weren't buying it. We had gone down this road before and knew we had to remain firm, no matter what Bronson said about us or his ability to return home. The most important lesson we had learned from the experience with Austin was that it wasn't about us. We couldn't make Austin better; only he could do that. "I can control most situations," I reminded myself, "but not this one."

I knew we'd taken Bronson to the right place as soon as I started talking to Barry Fell. Even before he got to know our son, he described Bronson's issues to a T. Most troubled teens, Barry told us, begin their descent after failing to meet expectations, either their own or their family's. Eventually, their anxiety overwhelms them and they are sucked into a depression, highlighted by low self-esteem. Eventually, they can't cope with the everyday tasks required to get through life. They try to keep their heads above water through self-medication, overeating, oversleeping, and overindulgence in technology, particularly gaming and social media. Barry said he sees kid after kid with stress-induced anxiety based on self-esteem issues. They're riddled with doubts, insecurities, and social anxiety. He was painting a perfect picture of Bronson.

Barry identified for us two of the primary causes of anxiety in teenagers. First, many of the students at Telos had struggled in mainstream schools because of difficulty processing new information. The way they learn best didn't align with the way their schools tried to teach them. Barry likens it to trying to load MAC software into a PC computer.

The other cause of anxiety for so many teens stems from an extremely competitive academic environment. If your child isn't taking every advance placement course and participating in every available extracurricular activity, they're made to feel like failures. Most kids get their sense of self by comparing themselves to their peers. When everyone around them is high-achieving, it makes them feel inadequate. They feel they need to stand out in order to be somebody. The pressures are kept inside—until one day they burst.

Parents often worsen the situation when they equate their child's worth with the college acceptance letters they receive. Bill and I were not blameless. It can't be easy being raised by two Type A personalities. As parents, we can be intimidating. We only want the best for our kids, but sometimes we don't go about it the right way. We've learned to back off. Avery, our youngest, has probably benefitted the most, although maybe her equanimity is more about her God-given personality than anything we've done. Then again, when you have six children, you're bound to get it right eventually.

Family Affair

When one of your children is in jeopardy, it becomes a family concern. During an emotional family weekend, we asked Avery if there was anything she wanted to say to Bronson.

"Why couldn't you just say no to the drugs?" she asked.

Simple, right? Just say no. But, of course, it's not simple at all. Bronson told her he couldn't figure out how to say no, that there were so many things going on in his life and in his mind that it never occurred to him that "no" was an option. Bronson and Avery both broke down in tears. But it wasn't sad; it was beautiful.

All this was a wake-up call for Bill and me. During a visit with Riley, our middle son, a senior at Lehigh University at the time, we talked to him about what Bronson was going through. Riley admitted that he, too, was feeling stress and anxiety. He was terrified he wouldn't meet his father's expectations.

"I know I've been tough on you through the years," Bill told him, "but honestly, it's more about you than me. We just want you to be healthy."

Hearing his dad say that was exactly what Riley needed. He broke down in tears as the relief washed over him.

Austin was involved with Bronson's therapy too. During their frequent phone conversations, he tried to pass along a simple message: "This is horrible now, but you're going to come out okay."

Austin spoke from experience. In 2007, after several months in

Cambodia, he returned to Texas somehow freed from his demons. He earned a theatre arts degree from St. Edward's University and began acting on stage and in movies. His first big break was a role in Richard Linklater's *Everybody Wants Some!!* In 2015, he was cast as Dwight in the television series *The Walking Dead.* More importantly, he's stable and happy, with a five-year-old son.

Bronson Comes Home

After a year and a half in Utah, Bronson returned home. He has gained valuable insights into his own behavior, as have I. Young people today are expected to be high achievers, but many of them haven't acquired the resilience they need to get there. Because you can order just about anything with a touch of a button (and a credit card), they expect instant gratification. If they're interested in something, they want it *now.*

This works alright when you're ordering a pizza from Domino's or buying a bongo drum on Amazon, but it's not the best way to achieve personal growth. Whether it's doing well in school or being a good friend, success requires hard work and patience. You can't learn the contents of a textbook by shoving it under your pillow and hoping to absorb the information. Many students have been conditioned to believe that if they can't achieve high marks with little or no effort, such marks aren't worth attaining. Instead of challenging them to try harder, any obstacles placed in their way create anxiety and fear.

Social media plays an enormous role in every teen's life, for good and ill. On the one hand, for those who become overly anxious in social situations, connecting with someone in the cyber world is far more comfortable than speaking to someone in person. You can have what appears to be a rich social life without ever having to leave your home.

On the other hand, technology can be just as effective at isolating people as it is at connecting them. Most kids gain a sense of self by comparing themselves with their peers, a tendency that nearly always leaves them feeling inadequate. When your self-worth is measured by comparing your humdrum existence to that of someone who has an impossibly large number of "friends" and a seemingly endless supply of photos depicting what appears to be a charmed life, you are sure to feel like a loser. Everyone is happy and well-adjusted on Facebook—or so it seems.

Telos has created a course called Connection Coaching. It teaches students how to feel comfortable enough inside their own skin to cultivate relationships in the real world. They are taught how to redefine their relationship with their phones, and they learn about metacognition—being aware of their own thoughts and learning how to process them.

Some students at Telos have issues with addiction, although that wasn't Bronson's primary problem. The school uses an adolescent addiction recovery method called the Seven Challenges model. It looks at the decision-making process from a teen's perspective, encouraging them to be honest with themselves about why using drugs feels so great in the moment, while at the same time understanding why it's so harmful.

Challenging Myself

After Bronson had been at Telos a few months, I was asked to speak to a group of parents who were thinking about sending their children there. I welcomed the opportunity because I understood exactly how they were feeling. When you're forced to make the decision to send your child away, you're tapped out emotionally and feeling desperate. You want to do what's best for your child, who is probably extremely resistant to the idea of going to a therapeutic school in the middle of nowhere. To follow through and do it, you must be brave.

My past experiences had empowered me. I was able to tell the parents I knew exactly how they were feeling because twice I had dealt with a suffering teenager. I think the fact that Austin had successfully come out the other side reassured many of them. We all agreed, "If we can just get them past high school, they'll be okay."

Talking to these parents was the first time I felt I could make a difference by sharing my knowledge about the mental health of teenagers. At this point, devoting more of my time or energy to this issue was just a germ of an idea. But I reminded myself that the origins of CFC were just as humble: I gave Srelin a dollar so she could go to school for a day because the idea she might not otherwise be able to attend bothered me. Lake Travis High School's failure to give Bronson the help he needed bothered me as well. But in this case, would I stay bothered long enough to do something about it?

After dedicating the previous sixteen years of my life to improving the education system in Cambodia, becoming consumed by the issue of teen mental health might seem like a major shift. But the two ventures aren't so different. They're connected by a common theme: helping children. This was nothing new for me. When Bill and I lived in Los Angeles in the 1990s, I served on the board of directors of Vistas for Children, which helps at-risk children find food, shelter, and healthcare and "adopts" individual families in need. I helped found Junior Vistas, which gave the children of volunteers the opportunity to get involved as well.

My mission to improve teen mental health in my corner of the world obviously sprang from a desire to get Bronson the help he needed. Getting healthy and staying healthy is going to be a lifelong process for him—just as it is for all of us. He still gets caught up in playing the blame game, and he can be stubborn to a fault. But he has made tremendous strides. He has a greater understanding of his anxiety and has become much better at controlling it. I also think he feels better not having all that THC inside him. He's developed important skills, such as "emotional regulation and distress tolerance"—which translated into English is the ability to manage intense emotions and deal with discomfort. Bronson and I are now intimately familiar with similarly cumbersome jargon, as well as a slew of acronyms such as CBT (cognitive behavior therapy) and ERP (exposure and response prevention).

Progress can be slow. When Bill and I visited Bronson at Telos the first time, he told us, "I hate you guys for doing this." By the time we left, he had amended that to "Okay, well, I hate you *temporarily*." Each day that passes gets better, and I truly believe that one day he's going to look back on his time at Aspiro and Telos and say that it was good for him and that he's grateful we sent him there.

With Bronson still in Utah, I found myself unable to shrug off the role the Lake Travis Independent School District (LTISD) had played in his declining health. I believe there are three pillars essential for successfully raising a child: parents, school, and community. I was taking responsibility for my role in Bronson's decline, but I don't believe his school had been sharing in that culpability. Clearly, it had failed him.

Angry with the LTISD for not even being aware of Bronson's problems and hoping to prevent such neglect from harming another child, in September 2017 I wrote a long email to Gordon Butler, the high school principal. Its purpose was not to assign blame; it was to inform him that my sensitive, creative, smart sixteen-year-old had somehow fallen through the cracks. Lake Travis could do better, I wrote. I pointed out that no one there had acknowledged—or even *noticed*—that Bronson hadn't been at school all year. I hadn't received a single call from a teacher, coach, or guidance counselor. It had been the same the previous year; no one from the school had reached out to us, even after Bronson had grown listless, anxious, and disinterested, and his grades had plummeted.

The school district's initial response was encouraging. It acknowledged that kids were falling through the cracks and that a better emotional support system was needed, particularly in the high school. The assistant superintendent seemed gung-ho about discussing what needed to be done. He encouraged me to join a committee that was looking into the problem.

By sending that email, I committed myself to a new project. You can't just complain about something unless you're willing to get out there and do something about it. I wasn't sure what I was getting myself into. I certainly had no end game in mind, but I agreed to get involved because I wanted to continue to educate myself about these issues. At one of the first meetings I attended, a policeman spoke about the large number of high schoolers doing drugs right under the noses of parents and teachers, and how an equally large number were surreptitiously "vaping" in class. At another meeting, Dr. Crystal Collier, director of the Behavioral Health Institute in Houston, gave a fascinating—horrifying, really—lecture about the adolescent brain. If you ever get a chance to hear her speak, you'll no longer shrug it off when your sixteen- or seventeen-year-old is smoking pot every weekend. The amount of THC in today's marijuana is at least three times as strong as it was just a few years ago, and its effect on the teenage brain is scary. It stunts the brain's development, and in many cases the damage is irreversible.

After my initial optimism that the LTISD shared my commitment to improving the emotional support system at the high school, I hit a brick wall. In response to a letter I wrote to the district superintendent, I received nothing but a form letter. It quickly became apparent they were stonewalling my suggestions, which included making drug testing mandatory for some students, establishing a more robust anxiety-recognition curriculum, and hiring a full-time psychologist. Lake Travis High School has only five counselors for thirty-five hundred students, and all five are *academic* counselors. The school has a million-dollar football stadium and a head coach who makes six figures. Surely we can afford a counselor devoted to the students' mental health and social well-being. What are we waiting for? Hopefully, not a tragedy at one of the schools in the district.

A big part of the problem is that LTISD, like so many communities, has swept its problems under the rug. It mostly buried a 2017 survey showing that nearly two-thirds of the students at Lake Travis High School agreed with the statement, "A lot of kids at school drink alcohol." More than two-thirds said they feel disconnected from their teachers, and a third said they feel pressured to drink or take drugs. Other red flags included high levels of anxiety and stress, and students harming themselves as a coping strategy. Most shocking was that despite a low response rate, thirty middle schoolers said they had attempted suicide in the previous twelve months. Thirty! That's astounding—and scary.

Much of the survey results mirror those found in the rest of the country. According to the U.S. Centers for Disease Control and Prevention, the suicide rate for young girls is currently at its highest level in forty years.

The Lake Travis school board promises that a much more comprehensive survey is in the works. Let's hope so—and that the results are quickly made public and an action plan put in place.

I'm not holding my breath. At a school board meeting I attended, the agenda was focused on honoring the board members and the incoming purchasing director and congratulating high school seniors for their many accomplishments. When it was time for public comment, I didn't stay silent. "We failed my son," I said to the room. "As parents, as a community, and as a school, we failed to see the signals when he walked into school a little more depressed and anxious than the day before. When he sat alone at lunch, no one noticed. I know there are many kids in the high school right now going through precisely what he did. They are stressed. They turn to drugs to numb their feelings. I am standing here tonight because I believe that with education and support, our kids can be emotionally healthier."

Members of the school board clearly did not want to hear from a concerned parent warning them about a problem they knew existed but didn't want to talk about. But I plowed ahead. I pointed out that Texas schools are required to have three universal prevention programs, and here it was already late January and the high school had yet to put even one in place. I observed that CFC's schools in Cambodia provided more emotional support than the ones in Lake Travis.

Needless to say, I've become frustrated by the maddeningly slow pace of change. The challenge for parents is getting our kids out of high school safely and equipping them with coping mechanisms so they stay healthy once they're on their own. But there are numerous students at Lake Travis who are emotionally and socially inept, who don't have a support system to rely on, and who are slipping below the waterline right under their parents' noses.

I know from experience how easy it is to ignore a problem with your son or daughter and simply hope it will go away. Parents need to take responsibility for their role in this growing crisis. One of the best things a parent can do is to create healthy and reasonable expectations and understand that a child's worth should not be measured by how well he or she performs in school. It's also important that parents educate themselves on this subject. If you can't differentiate between typical teenage behavior and a cry for help, you should learn.

At the end of the 2017–18 school year, when the LTISD finally released partial results of the survey, it did take some limited action. It made random drug testing mandatory for students in grades seven through twelve who participate in school-sponsored extracurricular activities, and for anyone requesting a parking permit. However, no strategy was developed to address the most crucial questions. Why are so many kids taking drugs? How can they be helped?

I understand that a large public school can never match the hands-on treatment at a place like Telos, with its tiny student body and many highly trained mental health professionals. But we can do better. Identifying students who are stressed to the point of breaking, steering them toward someone to talk to, and encouraging alternate behaviors can be prioritized. I've heard a lot of talk from LTISD about how it will implement an action plan based on the results of the last survey, but I have yet to see any results, or any action.

In the meantime, I've challenged myself to stay bothered. What if all the teachers in the U.S. helped their students understand that they are normal even when they're feeling depressed or anxious? What if teachers made discussing these feelings part of the curriculum? What if teachers were empowered to say things like, "It's okay if you feel bad or if you feel like no one understands you"? And what if students felt comfortable opening up to their teachers or a counselor about their feelings?

This issue started off as a quest to help my son, but it's evolved into something greater. I don't feel as though I have much of a choice. After seeing the effectiveness of staying bothered on the problems that plague Cambodia's education system, I feel obligated to give teen mental health in the United States the same treatment. It's personal, but finding a bother and staying the course is *always* personal.

EPILOGUE

—◦◦◦—

SECRET REVEALED

It hadn't been an accident at all.

With tears running down my cheeks, I decided it was time to finally unburden myself of a secret I had kept for more than thirty-six years. I had never told a soul: not Virginia, not my parents, not Bill . . . not anyone.

I made the decision on March 10, 2018, not a day I recall with fondness. Funerals typically produce one of three different levels of heartbreak. The easiest to bear is the passing of someone who has led a long, fulfilling life, like my vibrant ninety-five-year-old Aunt Jo, who succumbed after a short illness. Others are more complicated. When a close friend or family member passes before their time, I tend to experience it through a lens of extremes—grief, mixed with a joyful celebration of life. The grief becomes easier to bear when a person has left their mark on the world and on those they left behind.

There is a third category, by far the worst, one I wish I never have to experience again: the crippling heartbreak after the passing of a child.

I met fifteen-year-old Keaton and his mother, Andra, in early 2004 when, like us, they were living in Singapore as expatriates. A talented designer and the founder of Keaton Designs, Andra accompanied me on one of my first trips to Siem Reap, where she painted a wonderful mural at our first school. Austin and Keaton, both wild teenagers, bonded during that trip, particularly over their shared passions: rollerblading and skateboarding.

Fellow Texans and close CFC friends, Andra and I were also connected by our interest in design. Even after she moved back to Texas, she was always there to help me. Andra and Keaton left Singapore and returned to the U.S. a few years before we did. Austin and Keaton stayed in touch through social media. As Austin traveled in and out of addiction and recovery, Andra and I regularly talked about the difficulty of raising boys and how helpless we often felt.

When Keaton was in a "down" period, he tended to withdraw and sometimes even disappear for a week or more. Still, mothers worry, and in March 2018, after she hadn't heard from him for several days, Andra became concerned. After repeated calls and getting no answer, she went to his apartment. She sensed he was inside, but when she knocked and rang the bell, there was no response. The police broke down the door and found Keaton hanging by a computer cord from the ceiling.

The funeral was held at Chijmes, the 1940s chapel in Dallas that Andra had turned into a boutique hotel and event venue. The location may have been beautiful and inspiring, but the afternoon was excruciating, despite the effort by Keaton's family and friends to turn the occasion into a celebration of his life. I hugged Andra as hard as I could, as if that might help ease her pain. She is so strong; remarkably, she led the service.

Confession

As I sat in the pew next to Bill and spoke to old friends and made new ones, I kept overhearing people wonder aloud, "What was he thinking? What could possibly have prompted the kind of profound despair that would make Keaton, who seemed to have everything to live for, to take his own life?" It was inexplicable.

But it wasn't inexplicable to me.

A week after Keaton's funeral, I confessed to Bill. I told him about my high school years, about how I had been an unhappy sixteen-year-old. I suppose I wasn't much different than most teenagers in Schertz, Texas—or anywhere else in America, for that matter. I probably *seemed* happy, spending the summer floating down the Guadalupe River, swimming in our backyard pool, or giving lessons to young children to earn spending money. In truth, I was sad and depressed. I turned to drinking for relief, thinking it would be fun and make me happy. Instead, it made me feel worse.

It was a difficult time. I was having problems at school. I wasn't meeting my parents' expectations. Some kids were spreading nasty rumors about me, and a group of "tough girls" constantly harassed me, something that had started back in seventh grade. "We're going to beat you up after school if you don't stop seeing Ruben," they'd tell me.

Their demands were ridiculous, but the girls scared me. The rumors, the looks, the name calling, the snide comments—it was exhausting. I was tired of having to defend myself. It didn't help that I was struggling with the fallout from a breakup with my high school boyfriend, dealing with a bipolar mother and a wayward sister, and trying to find myself as a teenage girl. My feelings of frustration, fear, and anxiety were normal, but I didn't know that. When you're sixteen, your brain doesn't have any sense of perspective.

Exacerbating my situation, I felt I didn't have a safe place to unburden myself. I couldn't share my despair with any of my friends. I didn't have a BFF. And while I loved my parents dearly, I never felt I could discuss my feelings with them. Instead, I kept them bottled up inside.

I blamed myself. A trained professional could have helped me understand that my feelings could be explained, but such a person wasn't available to me. Feeling increasingly isolated, I got to a point where I felt I couldn't take any more pressure. My sister had wounded my parents by getting pregnant when she was fifteen. We were a strong Catholic family, and that could not have been easy for them, particularly during that era in rural Texas. I didn't want to place an additional burden on them with the stress I was feeling. If only my current self could have gone back in time and told my teenage self, "This will be okay. You'll get through it." But, of course, that wasn't possible.

FM Road 1518 offered what felt to me like the perfect solution. If done right, no one would know what had really happened. I understood exactly what to do. I had already chosen the perfect tree and curve in the road. Seatbelts weren't mandatory in 1981, and airbags were part of a distant future. People would assume I drove too fast around the curve and lost control of my car. Happened all the time; why would anyone think differently?

For weeks, I rehearsed the drive leading up to the oak tree. Finally, after drill team practice, I decided that this was the day.

The first time I approached the tree, I couldn't bring myself to do it. I drove past, turned around, and asked God to stop me if this wasn't supposed to happen. He didn't.

I hurried before I could change my mind. Once my foot pressed the accelerator to the floor, I knew there was no turning back. With my hands gripping the wheel, I locked my elbows and drove as fast as the car allowed, going straight where the road curved and smashing head-on into the tree.

I spent eight days at the Fort Sam Houston Medical Center, battered but still breathing. It wasn't my time to go.

The "accident" had a surprising consequence. It made me fearless. One day soon after returning to Schertz's Samuel Clemens High School, I turned a corner in the hallway, and suddenly there was Luz Headley, calling me a little bitch. I threw my books down and went right at her. I pushed her, then punched her in the face. The halls were crowded, so we had an audience. Luz was significantly bigger than me, but I put her on the ground, and she didn't get up until I walked away. After that, no one messed with me.

I felt powerful, but still alone. Worse, I now carried a new burden. God forbid if someone found out what I had done on FM Road 1518.

I thought I would go to my grave with the secret. How many times have I joked about the "accident?" For thirty-seven years, I told people the sixteen-inch scar on my stomach was from not wearing a seatbelt, which was technically true. I just never added that I hadn't buckled it on purpose.

I'm encouraged that so many celebrities have recently admitted that they have struggled with mental illness to the point where they have sought help. I'm a CEO, a wife, and a mom, but I am by no means a perfect person. I've suffered from negative feelings, and at times I have wondered if I would ever come out the other side. If I've learned anything, it's that we aren't supposed to be happy all the time.

The scar on my stomach is a daily reminder that I managed to survive a difficult time, and that I've been rewarded with an incredibly full life. *That*, I decided, was the message I wanted to deliver to my family and a few select friends.

I told Bill my story over a tall glass of wine one Friday night. Once the weight of that burden, which felt as heavy as the Plymouth Road Runner I'd once driven off the road, was finally off my shoulders, I was emboldened to share my story with others. The next day, I told my high school friend Rick and my nephews Anthony and Nick.

When I called Austin and told him, he had the most wonderful response. "Mom, I look at you, and I think you don't do anything wrong. I'm beginning to realize you are human, that you have feelings and make mistakes too."

I confessed my secret to Bronson in a letter, which I also sent to Riley. I asked Bronson to read it with his therapist, since he was still at the school in Utah. I wanted him to know that I've had problems in my life, too, that it doesn't make you weird if you're overwhelmed by stress and anxiety. They affect everyone. What's important is to talk to someone before they push you to the brink. "I don't want you ever to think you can't get through something," I wrote. "Things are never that bad (they only feel like it). I thought I was crazy, but I wasn't. I just didn't have things worked out yet. I became stronger and fierce. I chose not to be a victim."

My experiences in Cambodia have taught me how quickly a life fraught with hardship can be turned around. During CFC's first year, I was standing outside one of our schools when I saw a little boy crawling along the dirt road. David wanted to attend school, but he had a clubfoot, among other medical issues, and he couldn't walk. One of our volunteers, an orthopedic surgeon, outfitted him with a special pair of shoes, and our teachers gave him additional help. Today David is running and playing with his peers. He is very smart. Who knows? Perhaps one day he'll be the one to find a cure for dengue fever or cancer.

David and Riley as young children

When I start to think like that, I'm inspired. It's the mindset I'm hoping readers of this book will adopt. The biggest problems that need to be addressed in our increasingly chaotic world are so immense and unwieldy, you have to look in front of your face to have any chance of fixing them.

I still haven't figured out exactly where this inspiration comes from or how to conjure it up. I do know if you allow yourself to be open to it, it will come; you will see it. And when you do, that's when the real work begins. Success doesn't come easily. It takes a lot of effort, and there will be many setbacks along the way. I promise you it will be worth it.

Of course, *staying bothered* can be overwhelming. I've reached the point of exhaustion many times, which is why you can't allow your bother to be all-consuming. I have other roles beyond the CEO of a nonprofit. I'm a wife, mother, sister, and friend. My life is full of joy. To be able to stay bothered for the long haul, you need to include in your life balance and choices. Every time I fly home from Cambodia, I remind myself, "I can feel hopeless because of the enormity of the task, or I can feel hopeful because we've already changed the lives of thousands of children and will be changing the lives of thousands more in the future." If the choice is between being positive or negative, I'm going to choose the positive every time. Regardless of the obstacles placed in our path, regardless of how much responsibility we'll be able to turn over to the Cambodian communities, I will *never* lose my bother about Cambodia; I will *always* be committed to the country's children and to CFC.

If you take anything from this book, it should be this: take a moment to decide what bothers you the most, do something about it, and don't let the feeling fade. Hold on to it as tightly and as long as possible. *Stay bothered.* If each of us can do that, together we'll make the world a better place.

APPENDIX 1

—⟞⟝—

FAQS

Feeling bothered can be uncomfortable. How does a person manage to live his or her life staying bothered all the time?

There is no perfect answer to this question. The best I can offer is to maintain your perspective. You're not going to solve all the problems in the world, or even in your own neighborhood. You have a life to live—a job, a family, other responsibilities. For me, it's an ever-changing balancing act.

At the same time, a serious commitment on the part of many *does* change the world. For some, it works to set aside a number of hours or a particular day of the week to volunteer for the cause of their choosing. Others will take on a specific task and follow it through to its completion. You'll have to figure out what works for you.

Above all, keep your head up. It doesn't help to dwell or wallow in the negativity. Rather, keep the bother close by, but keep your other life commitments close by as well. *Feel* the bother every day, all the time, to stay motivated. Take the time to celebrate and be grateful for the victories—large and small.

What do you think makes an effective CEO/director of a not-for-profit organization, or even the head of a movement?

For me, one of the most important aspects of being a CEO is pretty obvious: it's to build relationships with the people you work with. This has been especially important for us working in a foreign country, which requires an enormous amount of trust on both sides. You need to work on getting to know someone before you can ask anything from them.

Another lesson: don't start something if you can't or don't want to lead. You've got to assume that others are looking to you to get things off the ground, move things to a different level, or step in when there are problems. That said, be sure you are surrounded by like-minded and committed individuals. That way, you have a team with whom you can share responsibilities and tasks.

How does one go about starting a non profit organization, also known as a nongovernmental organization (NGO)?
I could write an entire book on this topic (maybe I will!), but here is a to-do list to get started:

- Choose a name.
- Create a board of directors. Think of friends and colleagues who share your passion, and those with particular skills you might need, such as the ability to fundraise.
- Draft by-laws (i.e., "laws" that will govern your organization).
- Search the internet for examples you can emulate.
- Incorporate your organization in a specific U.S. state. There are a number of online services that can do this for you, such as incorporate.com.
- Apply to the Internal Revenue Service for tax-exemption status, the most common being a 501(c)(3) designation. This will allow your organization to receive tax-deductible contributions. You will also need to apply to your state's tax authority for tax exemption.
- Create a website that explains the organization's goals and highlights achievements with inspiring stories.

In addition to a board of directors, what other assistance should I be looking for?

Reach out to like-minded friends and family members you can count on for assistance. Take stock of the people you know and recruit those who can help with specific tasks. Do you have a friend who is a website designer? A lawyer who can help with the proper filings and might be willing to work pro bono? A CPA who would help you with your tax-exempt status and keep the books? A professional fundraiser?

Do I actually have to create a nonprofit organization to raise and distribute funds?

Not necessarily. These days there are many crowdfunding websites that can be used to raise funds. Among the most popular are GoFundMe and Indiegogo, but be aware that these sites may not be able to accept tax-deductible contributions, and they typically take a percentage of each contribution. Another possibility is raising funds through a nonprofit fiscal agent, although they, too, will take a small percentage of any funds processed through them.

As a project develops, priorities inevitably change. I'm often asked if what I envisioned when I first started CFC remained the same, or did it shift as my knowledge about Cambodian education and the circumstances in the country changed.

While our overall goal has not shifted, our priorities have changed as we have become more knowledgeable. During the first year or two, we didn't know what we didn't know.

CFC's original goal was to provide much-needed school supplies to the students I met during my first few trips to Siem Reap, and then provide bicycles so they could get to school. Quickly, however, we realized that for an extremely modest sum, we could rebuild a school, or even build a new school with classrooms, real windows, a real floor, and a colorfully friendly vibe. Soon we began to understand that our teachers, partly due to the Khmer Rouge having murdered anyone with an education, had no idea what it meant to be a teacher. So we focused on teacher training. The following year, when we recognized that our students weren't learning because they were arriving to school hungry, we began to serve free breakfasts and lunches.

In other words, as new needs arose, we adapted. At the same time, we kept in mind our mantra of going deep, not wide, in order to avoid "charity creep." As much as we want to feed every Cambodian student, train every Cambodian teacher, and make every Cambodian school a twenty-first-century center of learning, we know this is outside our mandate and our capabilities.

Why Cambodia?

Another question I'm often asked, although not nearly as frequently as I was in CFC's early years, has to do with the country I chose to help. "Why are you dedicating yourself to Cambodian education when schools in the United States have so many problems?" "Why should I contribute there and not here?"

My standard answer is that helping a country in need helps to improve the world, and my hometown is the world. What's more, in Cambodia a small investment can pack a powerful punch. A single contribution, a single MAD trip to help build a school, or a single teacher training course has a tremendous impact in a country where the average annual household income is $1,100.

This more-bang-for-your-buck response is a little too antiseptic for some. What do I *really* think? Why have I dedicated fifteen years of my life to the welfare of Cambodian children? I have another, more personal answer: God put me there. He keeps my spirit in Cambodia even when I'm not there physically, and we're making a huge difference in a small, beautiful country.

What Happened to Srelin?

Once I've explained how CFC got started and how it evolved into what it is today, people often ask me about Srelin, the little girl whose request for a dollar helped me stay bothered about the education system in Cambodia. I wish I could say that sixteen years later CFC has had the profound effect on her life that it has had on so many others. Unfortunately, it hasn't worked out that way.

I had dinner with Srelin the summer of June 2017. The few hours we spent together were bittersweet. She listened excitedly as I told her she was the inspiration for all CFC had achieved. She giggled with joy when I told her we started with one primary school and 343 students,

Recent photo of Srelin and me

and since then, more than seventy-seven thousand students have passed through our schools.

There was clearly still a connection between us. I saw the same sparkle in Srelin's eyes I had seen the day I first met her. She was still full of hope, but it was a different kind of hope, one tempered by the hard facts of her life. To help support her family, she dropped out of school after the seventh grade. She now works at two different markets, selling T-shirts and tennis shoes. When I ordered a pizza for us for dinner, I had to show her how to eat it. She is twenty-two years old and has never eaten pizza!

Srelin represents both the promise and the challenge of Cambodia. Many CFC graduates are now working at local restaurants and shops, health clinics, and entrepreneurial start-ups. Some are attending college and graduate school. But many others are trapped in poverty's web. We know we're not going to save every child in Cambodia. Most families still don't place much value on females getting an education. Children, particularly girls, often drop out of school when they're very young to help support their families. Poverty is endemic and difficult to overcome. These are the realities, and after much handwringing, I've learned to live with them.

How Do You Do It All?

After people learn about the juggling act I perform every day, I'm often asked, "How do you do it all? How do you manage CFC's $1 million budget, tap fundraising resources in Austin and beyond, manage a thousand-acre ranch in the Texas Hill Country, exercise most mornings, write books, and raise six children?"

Relying on organizational tools is a huge help. My calendar has become essential. Finding empty slots on it is like playing a game of Jenga. As I pull items from the bottom, my tower grows ever taller—but it also becomes less stable. That means certain tasks might stay at the bottom and never be completed.

Making lists also helps. I color-code mine. I try to keep my lists small and manageable. Crossing items off one of my to-do lists is so satisfying, I often put "Make a list" at the very top of each one I create.

Who doesn't wish they could have just one more hour in the day? I haven't figured out how to make that possible, but I've learned some other useful tricks. I've become a much better delegator. I don't hover over my volunteers the way I did in CFC's early days, because I'm confident they will accomplish whatever it is they set out to do. I've learned to trust people within CFC to make important decisions on their own, something I would never have done sixteen years ago.

When Michael Dell was asked how he managed to continue working hard even as his company was falling apart around him, his answer was, "Because my name is on the wall." When I first heard that, it resonated with me. When CFC was struggling to find its footing during its early years, I often thought, *My name is up there too. I refuse to fail.*

I do have one secret. The most important reason I'm able to "do it all" is that, in all honesty, I don't. No one can. It takes a team, a network, a community.

Here's another secret: Out of all the things I do, I don't do everything perfectly, or even extremely well. Lord knows, I'm not a perfect parent, perfect wife, or perfect nonprofit CEO. While I think I do a pretty good job in each of these roles, I haven't mastered any of them. Fortunately, I don't expect the kind of perfection from myself that I used to, although that doesn't mean I don't strive for it. I aspire to do great things, but I probably only do some things very well and only a few things incredibly well. In the end, I can live with that.

Two more things: Sometimes you don't know what you don't know. So take the time to learn. Watch TED Talks, listen to podcasts, and emulate the leaders you admire. Read and take people's ideas and use them. If they've done the research, why reinvent the wheel? My favorites are *Brene Brown on Leadership and Vulnerability* (a TED Talk), and the books *The Anatomy of Peace* and *You Don't Have to Fix Everything*.

And finally, have a sense of humor about it all. Don't take life too seriously. You cannot change everything. Change something and keep on going.

APPENDIX 2

———⁂———

HELPFUL HINTS FOR REPATRIATION

As explained in chapter four, repatriation is not easy—something my friends and I learned firsthand when we returned to the United States after idyllic stints in Singapore. Some say it takes an expat a full year of experiencing holidays and other personal events before feeling fully reestablished back home. However, as noted in chapter four, according to an international moving company, "If it takes an expatriate six to twelve months to adjust to their host countries, a *re*patriate should expect the adjustment period to be twice that."

Moving anywhere—including back home—can be stressful, but while much has been written about becoming an expatriate in a foreign county, very little is available about coming home. Here are some helpful hints for repatriates to keep in mind.

Emotional Challenges

- Don't be surprised if you experience "reverse cultural shock" and emotional issues in adjusting to the return home. You might have emotional "ups and downs," and possibly even a lot of "downs."

- Expect to feel "homesick" for your foreign home.

- Seek advice from other repatriates so you understand you're not alone.

- Don't hesitate to get professional help if you're having more serious issues adjusting.

- As an expat, you were a stranger in a strange land and forced to adapt. Now that you're "home," you may not feel that same motivation to adjust to your new life. Fight that lethargy.

- As you plan your return, make note of what you missed about home, then focus on those fond memories as soon as you arrive.

- At the same time, try to reconnect to the "everything is a new adventure" attitude you felt when you initially went abroad.

- Immerse yourself with what you enjoy— family and friends, sports, religious activities, movies, TV series, music, books, art, etc.

- Visit restaurants and other cultural connections with the foreign land you've left. You might even find a "repat community," just as you once found an expat community.

- Don't expect family or friends from your past to understand what you're going through, or even to be terribly interested in hearing about your foreign adventures.

- Your expat experiences have undoubtedly profoundly changed you as a person, but don't assume your friends back home have stayed the same either. Try to focus on their changes, as well as your own.

- Try to keep yourself busy and begin a new life for yourself.

Practical Suggestions

Cell Phone

Set up a new U.S. cell phone plan, but also set up a Skype, WeChat or similar free service so you can stay in contact with your friends in foreign countries.

Housing: Buy or rent?

While we lived in Singapore, we maintained ownership of a home in Texas, where we stayed during holidays and summers. As a result, in some ways for us the transition back home was easier than most. Otherwise, you might want to rent until you get your sea legs and have time to research best neighborhoods, schools, and so on.

Furniture

When the moving van finally arrived with our literal boatload of furniture from Singapore, all I could think was, "Why did I send so much back to the States?" Now that it's been almost nine years, I still have that same feeling! Of course, there are those irreplaceable items I am happy to have, but as much as you can, be a minimalist.

Taxes

Speak to your accountant, because it can be complicated. While out of the United States, you likely qualified for the Foreign Earned Income Exclusion (FEIE) and perhaps foreign housing deductions. Determining partial year deductions and how moving back to the United States will impact your tax status will likely require professional help.

Individual states, of course, have their own tax requirements. Although you may have not lived there for many years, states can use a variety of criteria to decide whether you have remained a resident during your time abroad, including your driver's license, voter registration, local bank accounts, bills, and properties owned or rented. Again, check with your accountant and/or state tax office before declaring yourself free and clear of tax state burdens.

Healthcare

There are so many rules these days about health insurance, you really need an expert to review them with you. Changes you might notice from the last time you lived in the U.S. include:

- An abundance of urgent care facilities that typically do not have the long waits typical at hospital ERs.

- Concierge medicine practices, where patients pay a monthly or annual fee for VIP services such as immediate text messaging, same-day access to a doctor, unlimited office visits with no co-pay, and a focus on preventive care.

- The growth of nurse practitioners and physician assistants. They have similar job descriptions as the physicians who oversee their work.

Food and Culture

America has become a foodie society! Food trucks, tapas (small portion dishes, not only Spanish food), and mixed international cuisines are now the norm. It started with Asian fusion restaurants, and now has spread across all ethnicities.

Traditional televisions are being replaced by Smart TVs, which can stream anything and everything. Devices such as Apple TV and Roku and services such as Netflix, Amazon Prime Video, Hulu, and SlingTV now compete with the cable and satellite TV you remember.

Of course, one's entire house can become a smart home, from lighting and vacuuming to lawn watering. Someday soon robots will be cooking and serving meals, just like in *The Jetsons*.

Sports teams are still sports teams, though new ones have arrived on the scene, such as the Las Vegas Knights, who stole the hearts of everyone during their inaugural 2017 season. In the NFL, the Oakland Raiders are also moving to Vegas.

APPENDIX 3

PLAYLISTS ON THE ROAD TO STAYING BOTHERED

As I mentioned in chapter five, music helps me feel the thoughts I may not know I have. The following are playlists I used to inspire me while writing each chapter.

Think Outside the Box
Prologue

"I Miss You"
Adele

"All on Me"
Devin Dawson

Take Me to Church
Hozier

"Chocolate"
The 1975

"Shots—Broiler Remix"
Imagine Dragons

"Good Grief"
Bastille

"Tongue Tied"
Grouplove

"Tilted"
Christine and the Queens

Make Your Own Rules
Chapter 1

"Brighter Than the Sun"
Colbie Caillat

"Don't Stop Me Now"
Queen

"Gotta Be Somebody"
Nickelback

"Viva La Vida"
Coldplay

"Rise Up"
Imagine Dragons

"If I Could Turn Back Time"
Cher

"Freedom! '90"
George Michael

"Bitter Sweet Symphony"
The Verve

"Don't Stop Believing"
Journey

"Life's Been Good"
Joe Walsh

"More Than a Feeling"
Boston

"Fallin'"
Alicia Keys

"American Pie"
Don McLean

"Story of My Life"
One Direction

"Carry On"
Fun

"Never Seen Anything
'Quite Like You'"
The Script

"People Like Us"
Kelly Clarkson

"1234"
Feist

Follow Your Intuition
Chapter 2

"Life's About to Get Good"
Shania Twain

"Never Comin Down"
Keith Urban, Shy Carter

"I Found Someone"
Cher

"Head Above Water"
Avril Lavigne

"Body Like a Back Road"
Sam Hunt

"Somebody Like You"
Keith Urban

"That's What I Like"
Bruno Mars

"The Cure"
Lady Gaga

"Something Just Like This"
The Chainsmokers, Coldplay

"Someone New"
Hozier

"Dare You to Move"
Switchfoot

"Inner Demons"
Julia Brennan

"Say Something"
Justin Timberlake, Chris Stapleton

No Giving Up
Chapter 3

"Dancing Through the Fire"
Jordan Feliz

"Setting the World on Fire"
Kenny Chesney, Pink

"Hell No"
Ingrid Michaelson

"Fresh Eyes"
Andy Grammer

"Water Under the Bridge"
Adele

"Still Falling for You"—Jonas
Blue Remix
Ellie Goulding, Jonas Blue

"Pieces"—Sam Feldt Remix
Rob Thomas, Sam Feldt

"It Girl"
Jason Derulo

"Misery"
Gwen Stefani

"Bulletproof Picasso"
Train

"Side to Side"
Ariana Grande

"Nobody"
Selena Gomez

"Over the Moon"
Cher Lloyd

"Walking in the Wind"
One Direction

"Superman (It's Not Easy)"
Five for Fighting

"You Give Love a Bad Name"
Bon Jovi

Follow Your Heart
Chapter 4

"Come On Get Higher"
Matt Nathanson

"Love Me Like You Do"
Ellie Goulding

"These Dreams"
Heart

"Truly"
Lionel Richie

"I Know You Were Waiting
(for Me)"
George Michael

"Because You Loved Me"
Celine Dion

"Unfaithful"
Rihanna

"Gravity"
John Mayer

"All I Ask"
Adele

"With or Without You"
U2

"I Don't Want to Miss a Thing"
Aerosmith

"Tainted Love"
Soft Cell

"Love on the Weekend"
John Mayer

"Put Your Records On"
Corinne Bailey Rae

"When You Say Nothing at All"
Boyzone

"Just the Way You Are"
Bruno Mars

"I Think I'm in Love"
Kat Dahlia

Keep Sharing, Keep Caring
Chapter 5

"Who Says You Can't Go Home"
Bon Jovi, Jennifer Nettles

"Last Day of School"
Boston

"Jack & Diane"
John Mellencamp

"Old Time Rock and Roll"
Bob Seger

"Someday"
Boston

"Centerfold"
The J. Gelis Band

"Cool Changes"
Little River Bends

"Hold on Loosely"
38 Special

"Love Bites"
Def Leppard

"Let Me Take
You Home Tonight"
Boston

"Time for Me to Fly"
REO Speedwagon

"Ramblin' Gamblin' Man"
Bob Seger

"Jamie's Cryin'"
Van Halen

"Amanda"
Boston

"The Heart of the Matter"
Don Henley

"Take Me Home Tonight"
Eddie Money

"The Flame"
Cheap Trick

"You Gave Up On Love (2.0)"
Boston

"My Best Friend's Girl"
The Cars

"Can't Fight This Feeling"
REO Speedwagon

"Turn the Page"
Bob Seger

"Magdalene"
Boston

"Hurts So Good"
John Mellencamp

"The Joker"
Steve Miller Band

"Animal"
Def Leppard

"Don't Do Me Like That"
Tom Petty and the Heartbreakers

"Keep on Loving You"
REO Speedwagon

"I Need Your Love"
Boston

"Kingdom Come"
Sebastien Izambard

You Can Do This
Chapter 6

"Edge of Seventeen"
Stevie Nicks

"I Love Rock 'n Roll"
Joan Jett & The Blackhearts

"One Way or Another"
Blondie

"Zombie"
The Cranberries

"What's Up?"
4 Non Blondes

"Hit Me With Your Best Shot"
Pat Benatar

"Piece of My Heart"
*Big Brother &
The Holding Company*

"Don't Wanna Fight"
Alabama Shakes

"Blood in the Cut"
K. Flay

"The Wire"
HAIM

"Celebrity Skin"
Hole

"Back to Black"
Amy Winehouse

"You Oughta Know"
Alanis Morissette

"Dog Days Are Over"
Florence + The Machine

"Because the Night"
Patti Smith

"I Hate Myself for Loving You"
Joan Jett & The Blackhearts

"Barracuda"
Heart

"You're So Vain"
Carly Simon

"Dreams—Dreams"
Fleetwood Mac

"Ex's & Oh's"
Elle King

"Shut Up and Let Me Go"
The Ting Tings

"I Put a Spell on You"
Annie Lennox

Staying Focused
Chapter 7

"I Knew You Were
Waiting (for Me)"
George Michael, Aretha Franklin

"Don't Speak"
No Doubt

"Stop and Stare"
OneRepublic

"Shallow"
Lady Gaga, Bradley Cooper

"Love Song"
Sara Bareilles

"Put Your Records On"
Corinne Bailey Rae

"All of Me"
John Legend

"Speechless"
Dan + Shay

"No One"
Alicia Keys

"What Lovers Do"
Maroon 5, SZA

"Pillowtalk"
ZAYN

"Slow Hands"
Niall Horan

"Music to My Eyes"
Lady Gaga, Bradley Cooper

"Chained to the Rhythm"
Katy Perry, Skip Marley

"Spiritual"
Katy Perry

"Fallin' For You"
Colbie Caillat

"Still Believe in Crazy Love"
Ryan Kinder

Courageous and Bold
Chapter 8

"Under Pressure"
Queen

"I Will Follow You
Into The Dark"
Death Cab for Cutie

"Slow Dancing in
a Burning Room"
John Mayer

"Only Love"
Ben Howard

"Let It Go"
James Bay

"Empire State of Mind" (Part II)
Alicia Keys

"Kiss Me"
Sixpence None The Richer

"Her Diamonds"
Rob Thomas

"Somewhere Only We Know"
Keane

"I'll Be"
Edwin McCain

"Wanted"
Hunter Hayes

"Life's What You Make It"
Graham Colton

"Every Morning"
Sugar Ray

"That Year's Love"
David Gray

"I Hope You're Happy"
Blue October

"I'm Still Here"
Vertical Horizon

"Soul Soul Soul"
Jack Johnson

"Everywhere"
Michelle Branch

"Used to Be"
Matt Nathanson

"True"
Ryan Cabrera

"God Gave Me You"
Dave Barnes

"Suddenly I See"
KT Tunstall

"You and I"
Ingrid Michaelson

"Two Is Better Than One"
Boys Like Girls, Taylor Swift

"Looking Up"
SafetySuit

"She's the Song"
Nathan Angelo
"3AM"
Matchbox Twenty

"Love Like This"
Natasha Bedingfield

"Time of Our Lives"
Tyrone Wells

"Free Fallin'"
John Mayer

"Peace"
O.A.R.

**Keep On Keeping On
Epilogue**

"Something 'Bout You"
Sir Roosevelt

"Beautiful"
Bazzi, Camilla Cabello

"The Ocean"
Mike Perry, SHY Martin

"Rich & Sad"
Post Malone
"Fantasy"
Alina Baraz

"High on Life"
Martin Garrix, Bonn

"Drew Barrymore"
Bryce Vine, Wale

"Fall for You"
Leela James

"Trip"
Ella Mai

"One Kiss"
Calvin Harris, Dua Lipa

"Beyond"
Leon Bridges

"Heaven"
Kane Brown

"Ball For Me"
Post Malone, Nicki Minaj

"The Middle"
Zedd, Maren Morris, Grey

"Demons"
Imagine Dragons

"Location"
Khalid

"All on Me"
Devin Dawson

"Good Life"
OneRepublic

"If I Told You"
Darius Rucker

"Takin' Shots"
Post Malone

"Promises"
Calvin Harris, Sam Smith

"Dance With My Father"
Luther Vandross

"Better Than I Used to Be"
Tim McGraw

"Broken Whiskey Glass"
Post Malone

"Are You with Me?"
Easton Corbin

"I R L"
DYSN, Prelow

"Breathin"
Ariana Grande

"Thunder"
Imagine Dragons

"Make You Feel"
Alina Baraz, Galimatias

"Feeling Good"
Michael Buble

"Lost in You"
Erick Morillo

"Black"
Dierks Bentley

"Someone Like You"
Adele

"Walking the Wire"
Imagine Dragons

"I Think of You"
Easton Corbin

"Don't Leave"
Snakehips, MO

"Beautiful Crazy"
Luke Combs

"Never Be the Same"
Camila Cabello

"The Bravest"
Sir Roosevelt

"Redbone"
Childish Gambino

"Tonight (Best You Ever Had)"
John Legend, Ludacris

"The Cute"
Stevie Parker

"River"
Leon Bridges

"Beautiful Mess"
Diamond Rio

"Natural"
Imagine Dragons

"Home"
Michael Buble

"Made to Love"
John Legend

"It Goes On"
Zac Brown, Sir Roosevelt

"Can I Be Him"
James Arthur

"Across the Room"
ODESZA, Leon Bridges

"Make You Miss Me"
Sam Hunt

"If Only for One Night"
Luther Vandross

"Waterfalls"
TLC

"Born to Be Yours"
Kygo, Imagine Dragons

"Everytime"
Ariana Grande

"Girls Like You"
Maroon 5, Cardi B

"Who Do We Think We Are"
John Legend

"Always Remember Us This Way"
Lady Gaga

"Bright"
Echosmith

A DECADE OF LIFE

AMELIO FAMILY CHRISTMAS CARDS
2007–2018

Every year I reflect on the previous twelve months
and try to convey the voyage our family has taken.
The Christmas cards I send out each year tell that story.

Christmas 2007

Snowflakes might seem like an odd motif for a family living in Singapore, where it has never, ever snowed. But I associate Christmas with winter, and I was using snowflakes as a metaphor for floating away.

On the cover on the top right is our youngest, Avery, from a photo I snapped in church on Easter Sunday. All the pictures are actually paintings, made from photos I sent to Dallas artist Christina Keith, who was on an expat assignment in Singapore.

Top of mind as I put this card together is our eldest, Austin, who had been through the ringer. I am desperately hoping he will emerge healthier and wiser. The picture of the two of us on the bottom right is from the day I dropped him off at college in Los Angeles, many miles from our home in Singapore. I have my fingers crossed. "Wherever the wind carries you, we wish you peace," I am telling him. He is on his own journey now; I am letting him go. "Life is not about finding our place in the world, but making it."

The snowflakes also represent traveling the sky, the world. Riley, Bronson and Avery are in Cambodia; Rathana and Cherry are in the pool at the American Club in Singapore; Avery is at home in Texas;

Austin and Bronson are in San Antonio, and Riley, Cherry, and Rathana are at SAS, the Singapore American School. Bill is holding Avery.

Austin and Bronson with a basketball are in San Antonio after we sat with NBA Commissioner David Stern courtside at a Spurs game, my hometown team. Bill is still with Lenovo, which was doing a promotion with the NBA. Boy, was that fun, although I have mixed feelings when I look at the picture of Rathana, Cherry, and Riley in basketball jerseys. Just after I snapped it, I was coaching Rathana and she was so rude to me that I had to send her out of the gym. I look at that picture and go, "Grr," but then I smile when I think of the other moments reflected in these paintings. "The moments we live are like the sparkles in the stars; the memories we make are like the snowflakes in the wind."

Christmas 2008

In 2008 we are in the groove. Bill and I still have some issues with Rathana, but we are better prepared to help her with them.

This is the first summer the girls come home to Texas with us, although in the group picture, we are in Singapore. We're playing cards in our living room in Austin; the kids underwater are at that house too. The other photographs were taken at Angkor Wat.

Somehow, putting all the photos in sepia makes them feel more real

to me. The two group pictures say a thousand words, so I placed the one of us all smiling on the front. Everyone looks so happy, and we are. Austin is twenty, and I'm feeling like he's getting there, which I can read in my smile. The summer of 2008 is when he and his cousin Nick go to Siem Reap and Austin begins to turn his life around. But there will always be more miles to travel.

"The story is this . . . we have come so far; we have so far to go."

We have come so far...

Season's Greetings

新年
快乐

The Amelio Family
Bill and Jamie

Riley 12   Austin - 20   Rathana 14   Cherry 12

Bronson 4 (8D)

Go in Peace.

Austin, Rathana, Cherry, Riley, Bronson, Avery. 3 1/2

Christmas 2009

"Today is a gift; that's why they call it the present." Sometimes clichés are just . . . true.

I am attempting to remain in the present. "Give your heart . . . being kind . . . give it away." I am really trying to live by this, but at the same

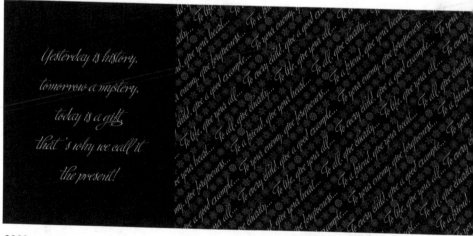

Yesterday is history,

tomorrow a mystery,

today is a gift,

that's why we call it

the present!

time not get too wrapped up in what I cannot control.

Bill is looking for a job, so we know we'll be returning to Austin. Be calm, I tell myself; everything will be fine. Bronson has come through his chin surgery, so that is a relief. Teenage girls are tough, but the others are doing great. Just look at them.

I am also feeling good about CFC. Natalie has accepted the challenge of taking over as president, so I know I am leaving CFC in good hands. Thank goodness for Skype.

Christmas 2010

We don't seem as happy on the 2010 card as we did in previous years. Looking at our smiles now, they seem a little forced. For good reason: this is the year Virginia died, which is why getting our Christmas card just right kept me up at night.

Every year, the cards are all me, as I try to create portraits that give meaning to our life during a particular twelve months. No one in the family questions what I have in mind. Each card has a theme, a mission. They aren't put together in a day.

The photos are more posed this year. Life feels very still. I'm searching, looking for what is in front of me, not behind. It is our first Christmas in Austin without Virginia. Bill is traveling a lot in his new job. Austin is living downtown.

Life is full of little tr

2010

The main photo, with everyone's back to the lake, is kind of weird, but it demonstrates how I feel: my back turned to life. So much is going on that I don't like; some days I just want to turn around. Virginia is behind us; we have to say good-bye.

Still, when I think I am sinking, I desperately look for something good. I try to find the little treasures, and there are many. Seven of them, in fact.

We are living on a lake, so that's the backdrop, but also because symbolically, water is the source of life itself, as in the story of creation when life emerges from primordial waters. Virginia is gone, but she lives through the Amelios.

Christmas 2011

All year I have the Christmas card in mind. It's my life story. People get these cards and say, "Oh, they're so nice," not thinking much about what went into them. There is so much of me that is behind them. I feel like I write a book every year.

These photographs were taken on Whistler Mountain, just north of Vancouver. When we lived in Los Angeles, we used to ski there. In those days, it was just me and my four boys—Bill, Austin, Riley and Bronson. Our family has grown.

Everyone seems balanced in these photos; at least that's how I want them to be. I made *balance* this year's theme, because that is my wish for the family.

We wish you the strength to look beyond the forest and see all the trees!

The Amelio Family
Bill and Jamie
Austin, Rathana, Cherry, Riley, Bronson & Avery

2011

As we climb further up the mountain, it turns to snow and we must all maintain our balance. Bronson is our best snowboarder; he never falls. Riley is focused and driven, as always. Avery is on the road less traveled, with Bill running after her and Cherry happily following behind. Austin on the log is so him. This is the year I am driving downtown during rush hour and see a crazy kid on a skateboard weaving through traffic. As I approach 12th and South Lamar, I realize it's *my* freakin' son. Very Austin; living on the edge.

Christmas 2012

Choose the lens through which you look at the world.

For our 2012 Christmas card, I choose the lens for each Amelio, but as I do that, I realize they have chosen it for themselves long ago. Maybe it's not a choice. Are we born the person we become? Nature or nurture? My children are so different from each other, with singular personalities. And Rathana and Cherry are first cousins, but night and day.

Still, the Christmas cards are my department, so I choose their lens for them. Kindness for Bronson. Perseverance for Riley. Laughter and love for Avery. Peace and tranquility for Cherry. Determination for Rathana. Risk for Austin.

And for all of us—belief.

For me, I tell myself to smell the roses, slow down and stop working so hard. While finishing *Graced with Orange* and trying to get the kids sorted, I'm also trying to have some fun.

This year, more than others, I am looking at life through a camera

· Choose kindness ·

· Choose persevera

· Choose laughter and love ·

· Choose peace and tranq

lens. I'm continually back and forth from Texas to Cambodia. Rathana is having a lot of trouble, and I so dislike the school the kids are attending in Austin. This is the year I attend their lacrosse and football games feeling isolated and alone.

I am trying to change the way I look at things. Choose kindness and perseverance, I keep telling myself. Smile and give it away, to everyone. Avoid people who do not reciprocate the kindness. Choose to believe in family, to look at Avery every day and see how happy and wonderful she is. Choose to see Cherry's serenity, and the boys' growing independence.

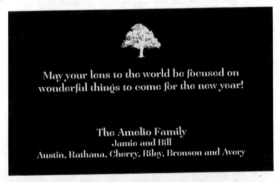

May your lens to the world be focused on wonderful things to come for the new year!

The Amelio Family
Jamie and Bill
Austin, Rathana, Cherry, Riley, Bronson and Avery

· Choose to believe ·

Choose the lens at which you look at the world

determination ·

· Choose risk ·

Christmas 2013

Our family is dispersing. I am trying to signal with the closed door how difficult it has become to get everyone together for a group photo. But after the deception is finally revealed that my most trusted Cambodian friends have been keeping from me for almost a decade, another door has closed.

CHERRY, 18

AUSTIN, 25 - ACTOR

EATHANA, 19 -GAP YEAR- CAMBODIA

BILL & JAMIE

BRONSON, 13

RILEY, 17

AVERY, 8½

We call this a *gap year* for Rathana, but really, she is in Cambodia to find perspective and work on herself. Cherry is, of course, at peace. We are loving the ranch, so most of the photographs are from there.

Good health, family, faith, love and laughter. Our recipe for a meaningful life. We hope you find all of this and more beyond the doors of the new year.

Season's Greetings

Bill, Jamie
Austin, Rathana,
Cherry, Riley,
Bronson and Avery

Good health, family, faith, love and laughter. Our recipe for a meaningful life. We hope you find all of this and more beyond the doors of the new year.

Season's Greetings

Bill, Jamie
Austin, Rathana,
Cherry, Riley,
Bronson and Avery

Christmas 2014

Joy to the world. That says it all. Our grandson, Lev, is born, and that makes us all smile. The font is bright, as are our faces. Austin and Riley have become young men. Rathana seems to be getting better, and is back in Texas working, at school part-time. Bronson is in middle school; Riley is a senior. It is a good year. I am making a concerted effort to see the good in others.

At the same time, I am starting to feel worn out. But I know I will never give up, so I just keep at it. I am wishing my friends "the strength that comes from a close family, the courage to see the good in others, and the ability to give a little more of yourself each day."

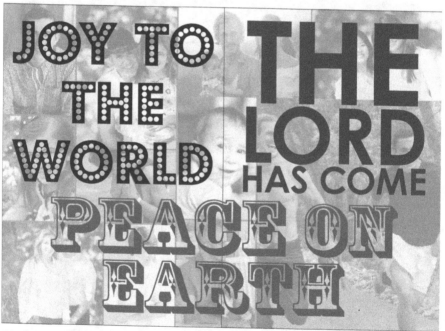

2014

We wish you the strength
from a close family...
the courage to see the good in
others and the ability to give a
little more of yourself each day.

Christmas 2015

"Write your own lyrics." I like that phrase. Just do it. Life is too short for all this serious stuff. Life *is* a song. Be who you want to be.

I have just seen myself die, so in these photos I am happy to be alive, feeling super blessed. I am turning fifty, celebrating with a party. This is the first year without Rathana. I'm singing my own song, writing my own lyrics, celebrating life, love, and faith with those I love.

2015

Riley loving college life at Lehigh University.

Bronson a freshman playing varsity lacrosse.

Avery in 5th grade loved dance and volleyball.

Cherry in her junior year as an honor student at University of Incarnate Word in San Antonio.

Rathana at Austin Community College.

Austin and Jes with beautiful grandson Leo.

Write your own lyrics...
Celebrate life, love and faith...
And then just dance!

✳

Happy New Year
with love
The Amelio's

We wish you a Merry Christmas;
We wish you a Merry Christmas;
We wish you a Merry Christmas
and a Happy New Year.

Christmas 2016

Family is like branches of a tree, growing outward but still connected. Serene in the good weather; strong even when it storms.

But the branches grow in different directions. Riley and Cherry are in college. Austin has moved to Atlanta, which is hard for me, but exciting.

Bill
forever rancher and new CEO at Avnet.

Jamie
CFC strong, and loving being Gigi.

Lev
2 1/2, full of life, loving dinosaurs and letting his imagination soar every day.

Austin
AKA... Dwight on The Walking Dead, AMC's hit TV series. He, Jes and Lev live in Atlanta.

Bill (Bull) and I (Gigi) have discovered the "grandparent" bug.

The
Wishing you bl
and good l
Happy New Ye

I feel grateful and happy. I haven't yet anticipated Bronson's problems. The branches grow as if they have a mind of their own, but we'll always be one big, loving family.

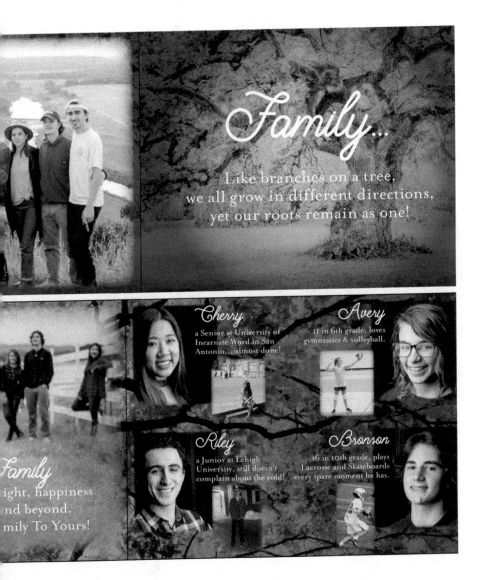

Family...

Like branches on a tree,
we all grow in different directions,
yet our roots remain as one!

Cherry
a Senior at University of
Incarnate Word in San
Antonio... almost done!

Avery
11 in 6th grade, loves
gymnastics & volleyball.

Riley
a Junior at Lehigh
University, still doesn't
complain about the cold!

Bronson
16 in 10th grade, plays
Lacrosse and Skateboards
every spare moment he has.

Family
ight, happiness
nd beyond.
mily To Yours!

Christmas 2017

I almost didn't make the printer's deadline for the 2017 card. I am consumed with events in my own life and around the world—with CFC, health issues, writing a book, the political discourse in Cambodia and America, keeping my own head on straight, and most of all, with Bronson. Two weeks after this group photo is taken, he is in Utah, finally on the right path. But I don't know that then, and I am worried.

Still, when I write the words that become the background of the front cover, I feel better, more optimistic. I may be anxious about democracy, health, failure, and daily challenges, but I am also buoyed by grit, tenacity, inspiration, compassion, drive, family, friends, faith, and love. There are more positives in my life than negatives, and I am grateful.

Yet I am troubled, mostly about Bronson. You can see the anxiety on his face. But now I look at the group photo, and the individual ones too, and I see happy people who, seemingly overnight, have become adults. Austin has a career, Cherry is in the workforce, Riley will soon be

Bronson, 11th grade and completed his first triathalon

Avery, 7th grade Volleyball is her sport

Our grandson, Lev A laugh a minute! 3 1/2

Austin, Jes and Lev living in Atlanta. Austin is still playing "Dwight" on The Walking Dead

Riley, a Senior at Lehigh University

Cherry, Graduating from University of Incarnate Word College with a BA in International Business and a Minor in Accounting

graduating college. Even thirteen-year-old Avery looks like a young lady. Lev is the only remaining child, and he keeps us all smiling. My grin only broadens when I see Bill—always the rock, the giver, the listener.

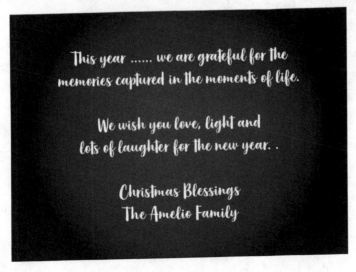

This year ...... we are grateful for the memories captured in the moments of life.

We wish you love, light and lots of laughter for the new year. .

Christmas Blessings
The Amelio Family

Christmas 2018

This year's card is all about simplicity. Sure, important family milestones occurred: Riley's college graduation, Cherry's employment, and Bronson's high school football prowess among them. Yet I didn't feel I had to individualize our accomplishments. We were healthy, happy, and positively moving forward, and that was more than enough. How we got there is well illustrated in the previous decade's worth of Christmas cards.

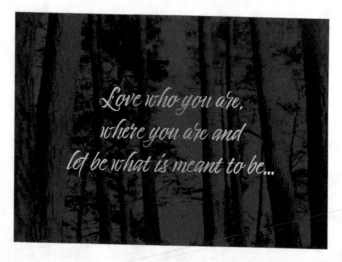

Love who you are, where you are and let be what is meant to be...

Merry Christmas and Happy New Year

*Wishing you the power
to find love and laughter
more than ever before.*

*Love,
Bill, Jamie, Austin, Jes, Lev,
Cherry, Riley, Bronson and Avery*

—⚬⚬⚬—

Be vulnerable and share your thoughts about your world,
in whatever form that feels right. One of my ways is to send friends
and family an annual Christmas card where I try to express my
feelings and appreciations for the previous year.

—⚬⚬⚬—

CPSIA information can be obtained
at www.ICGtesting.com
Printed in the USA
FFHW011620271119
56113867-62206FF

9 781948 181648